The Ethos of Black Motherhood in America

Lexington Studies in Health Communication

Series Editors: Leandra H. Hernández and Kari Nixon

National and international governments have recognized the importance of widespread, timely, and effective health communication, as research shows that accurate, patient-centered, and culturally competent health communication can improve patient and community health care outcomes. This interdisciplinary series examines the role of health communication in society and is receptive to manuscripts and edited volumes that use a variety of theoretical, methodological, interdisciplinary, and intersectional approaches. We invite contributions on a variety of health communication topics including but not limited to health commnication in a digital age; race, gender, ethnicity, class, physical abilities, and health communication; critical approaches to health communication; feminisms and health communication; LGBTQIA health; interpersonal health communication perspectives; rhetorical approaches to health communication; organizational approaches to health communication; health campaigns, media effects, and health communication; multicultural approaches to health communication; and international health communication. This series is open to contributions from scholars representing communication, women's and gender studies, public health, health education, discursive analyses of medical rhetoric, and other disciplines whose work interrogates and explores these topics. Successful proposals will be accessible to an interdisciplinary audience, advance our understanding of contemporary approaches to health communication, and enrich our conversations about the importance of health communication in today's health landscape.

Recent Titles in This Series

The Ethos of Black Motherhood in America: Only White Women Get Pregnant
By Kimberly C. Harper
Medical Humanism, Chronic Illness, and the Body in Pain: An Ecology of Wholeness
By Vinita Agarwal
Social Support and Health in the Digital Age
By Nichole Egbert and Kevin B. Wright
Narrative Journeys of Young Black Women with Eating Disorders: A Hidden Community among Us
By Stephanie Hawthorne
Unintended Consequences of Electronic Medical Records: An Emergency Room Ethnography
By Barbara Cook Overton
eMessaging and the Physician/Patient Dynamic: Practices in Transition
By Susan Wieczorek
Communicating Mental Health: History, Contexts, and Perspectives
By Lance R. Lippert, Robert D. Hall, Aimee E. Miller-Ott, and Daniel Cochece Davis
CTE, Media, and the NFL: Framing of a Public Health Crisis as a Football Epidemic
By Travis R. Bell, Janelle Applequist, and Christian Dotson-Pierson
Challenging Reproductive Control and Gendered Violence in the Americas: Intersectionality, Power, and Struggles for Rights
By Leandra Hinojosa Hernández and Sarah De Los Santos Upton
Politics, Propaganda, and Public Health: A Case Study in Health Communication and Public Trust
By Laura Crosswell and Lance Porter
Communication and Feminist Perspectives on Ovarian Cancer
By Dinah Tetteh

The Ethos of Black Motherhood in America

Only White Women Get Pregnant

Kimberly C. Harper

LEXINGTON BOOKS
Lanham • Boulder • New York • London

Published by Lexington Books
An imprint of The Rowman & Littlefield Publishing Group, Inc.
4501 Forbes Boulevard, Suite 200, Lanham, Maryland 20706
www.rowman.com

6 Tinworth Street, London SE11 5AL, United Kingdom

Copyright © 2021 by The Rowman & Littlefield Publishing Group, Inc.

All rights reserved. No part of this book may be reproduced in any form or by any electronic or mechanical means, including information storage and retrieval systems, without written permission from the publisher, except by a reviewer who may quote passages in a review.

British Library Cataloguing in Publication Information Available

ISBN 9781793601421 (cloth)
ISBN 9781793601445 (pbk)

Library of Congress Control Number: 2020944240

I dedicate this book to my children, Naeemah and Amir Khalfani.

Naeemah—should you choose to become a mother, may you live in a world that honors your needs as a Black woman and mother. I pray that your love for the arts will continue to nourish your soul and bring you joy. Remember our song, "I gotta be me; you gotta be you. No matter what the world may say, I gotta love me anyway." May your womanhood be shaped by YOUR vision for your life and not the world's, and when you need strength, turn to Allah—always. Ameen.

Amir—I pray that your world remains full of wonder and joy—much like it is now at age 5 and that you never stop seeking the goodness in life—even as you mature. Should you choose to become a father, I pray that you will resist the male narrative that says you cannot express love and emotions—for yourself or your child(ren). I pray that you will be able to grow up and thrive despite the world's very real and dangerous obsession with Black men in "so called" White spaces. May you always be grounded in faith and love, and when the world becomes too much or you need a break, I pray that you always turn to Allah for guidance. Ameen.

To mother means to resist and motherhood, although tiresome and demanding, is a beautiful manifestation of love. So, whatever I do in this world, I resist for myself, for you, and for our community.

I also dedicate this book to my mother Mrs. Betty H. Harper who has been engaged in resistance mothering for 81 years. She was my first teacher, stylist, confidante, protector, cheerleader, and has remained a constant support in my life and the lives of my children. Everyone should be so lucky to have such a dedicated mother. To my older sister Toni, who is my second mother, thank you. Because of you, I am. I went to college because you set the example. I will never forget the day my class went to the UNC-Chapel Hill Morehead Planetarium, and you stopped by and said, "hello" while we ate lunch outside. You, in your 1980s Blackgirl swag and cornrows with beads, walked through a plethora of elementary school kids to find me. I told the kids, "That's my big sister; she goes to school here." I was so proud, and all these years later, I am still proud.

Finally, I dedicate this book to all the mothers, othermothers, and fictive kin who continue to engage in their own form of resistance so that Black children may live and thrive.

Love always,

Kimberly

Contents

Acknowledgments ix

Introduction xi

1 Historical Representations of Black Motherhood 1
2 Setting the Tone 11
3 The Legislative Decisions Governing Black Wombs 23
4 Ideology, Ethos, and Silence 49
5 Where Are All the Black Mothers in Pregnancy Books? 65
6 Reproductive Justice and Black Women's Lives 75
7 Black Midwives and Reclaiming Choice 85
8 The Will to Resist Is a Form of Love 97

Conclusions 109

Appendix A: Level of Care Questionnaire 113

Appendix B: Emergency C-Section Stories. 117

Bibliography 119

Index 127

About the Author 135

Acknowledgments

As a social scientist and English professor, I recall being asked how I fit into a discussion that is squarely rooted in the medical field and related areas like public health. My response was that I mother my own children; I *other mother* students that come into my classroom, and I am fictive kinfolk to several women that I've crossed paths with who are also mothers. My traumatic birth experience, along with my understanding of the intersectionality of motherhood, gives me reason to press forward—not press pause. I do not say all of this to build credibility but to say that the work comes from many places and in many forms. As they say, love comes in many forms, and my form is that of a reproductive activist working to untangle some of the rhetoric that prevents Black mothers from having a voice.

This project came to life after the birth of my first child and has been with me the last eight years. I've grown, my children have grown, and, finally, I'm ready to set it free. I must first give thanks to Allah. Through this work I've found my purpose, and through this work I hope to do more for Black mothers and families in general. I do not call myself a feminist nor a womanist, but if I must identify with one term, it would be womanist because I am dedicated to the development of all people. As such, this book is about the needs and experiences of Black women, and for that I do not apologize.

I would like to thank my husband Shareef for his support and my brother Rodney for his encouragement. My father, Ronald E. Harper, did not live to see me complete this effort, but I would like to thank him for instilling in me the understanding that it's ok to walk your path alone and that broke people will make you broke ☺. I would also like to thank colleagues Dr. Hope Jackson and Mrs. Adri-Anne Jones—Mrs. Jones "I'm Black to the Core!" To my students who listened and encouraged me, thank you. To my close friends Dr. Daaiyah Saleem, Dr. Natasha Scott, Anitra McInnis, Robyn Abdusamad, Patrice Smith, Mentzi Abdul-Rahman, thank you for sending news clippings, asking about the project, and pushing me to finish. Thank you to Dr. Marva Banks who was my "other mother" when I became a mother. You stepped in and did what I know my mother would have done had we lived in the same state. To "other mothers" Donna Lynem, Jenise Abdul Razzaaq, and Amatullah Yamini, thank you for your dua'aa and for participating in my Black Maternal Health Conference. And to Jinaki Abdullah—thank you, thank you, thank you. You were right there in the trenches with me. Thank you for pushing me to the finish line!

Introduction

Prior to the arrival of my first child, I started looking for a pediatrician ahead of her birth. Like a dutiful new mom in training, I made sure to follow all the suggestions given to me by my prenatal provider. I researched and decided on three choices. My first choice had a two-year waiting list, so I went with my second choice. I showed up for my appointment eight months pregnant and was repeatedly asked about my employment and insurance. When the receptionist was satisfied I had proper coverage, she then asked me about my husband's employment and insurance. She pressed me for a secondary insurance. I told her that I carried our family because my insurance was better, and we did not have a secondary insurance. She finally acquiesced and allowed me to fill out the application; however, she continued to stress the importance of secondary coverage. I ended up taking the application home and telling the receptionist I would bring it back the next day. I never went back. That was my first brush with the intersection of race, class, and motherhood.

On my way to work one morning, I was pulled over for driving with expired license tags. The officer asked for my driver's license. I explained that my husband had forgotten to put the sticker on the tag. After confirming that my license plate was current, rather than allowing me to wait until I got to work, the officer made me get out of the car and place the sticker on the tag immediately. While doing this, she got in her car and pulled off. Here I was eight months (large) pregnant on a side street in the hot Georgia heat. I was flabbergasted that the officer, a woman, would insist that I put the tag on the car immediately. For some reason, I believed that my bulging belly would give me a reprieve. That was my second brush with the intersection of race, class, gender, and motherhood. During a prenatal visit, I casually mentioned that I was trying to make myself eat avocados because they are good for your pregnancy. The physician looked up and asked, "Who told you that?" My response was that I read it on a pregnancy blog, and my friend who was training to be a doula confirmed what I read. The physician agreed, but it was clear from her initial response that she was surprised.

On November 27, 2011, I was admitted to the hospital for the birth of my first child. I was not allowed to walk around while I labored, and then without discussion, the attending nurse/midwife started the process of inducing labor without informing me of the steps that she was taking. I did not know what to expect and my questions went unanswered. During labor I incurred several second-degree cervical lacerations, and I lost a lot of blood. I distinctly remember looking across the room and seeing the doctor pull my husband and mother into a private conversation as I held my newborn. He then explained to me that he needed the proper lighting of an emergency room in order to find and stitch all my wounds correctly. He was concerned that if he did not stop the bleeding, I would hemorrhage and suffer life threatening complications. I was later told that I had to have a blood transfusion due to the amount of blood loss.

As my mother so aptly stated after I came home from the hospital a week later, "What if you had lain in bed that night thinking, as a first-time mother, this much bleeding is normal after giving birth. Or what if you did not think it was normal, but the nurses dismissed your concerns and left you to bleed to death. They did not tell you anything about the process of induction and did not explain what was happening, so who is to say they would have taken your concerns seriously." I believe, as does my family, that the attending physician saved my life that night. However, after that experience, I was left with a dull pain in my left side for close to two years. I sought medical care with a new OB/GYN practice, and it was discovered that during the surgery a small part of my cervix had been sewn to the wall of my uterus when the doctor repaired my cervical lacerations. I was told that it would take time to separate on its own and I should wait at least a year before having another child. Despite the pain, I still think the doctor saved my life by insisting he repair my tears in the emergency room. Eventually I healed, the physical pain went away, and I had another child, but the emotional trauma lingered.

Three years after giving birth to my first child, I sat in our pediatrician's office on a lovely December day in 2014, dutifully answering "well-visit" questions regarding the newest addition to our family. When we came to the question about my son's wheezing and family history, I began to tell him that my oldest child suffered with eczema, but she did not have the pre-asthmatic symptoms that my son exhibited and that my husband and his siblings had a history of asthma. Without even looking up from his laptop, he casually asked me, "Same father?" I was astonished that he would ask such a question, especially since my daughter had been his patient since she was two. He met with my husband during several visits, and he had seen my daughter several times prior to the birth of my son. That was my third brush with the intersection of race, class, and motherhood.

As I walked out of his office, I started recalling all the little things that happened to me over the years. Then I started having the racial micro-aggression conversation that many African Americans have with their inner self when things like this happen. Did she quiz me about my insurance because I am Black? Did she think I could not afford private insurance? Did that cop make me get out of the car with my eight-month belly because I was a Black woman? Did the doctor ask me if my children had the same father because I am a Black woman? Had I been a White woman would these situations have played out differently? Would the receptionist have been satisfied with one insurance provider? Would the cop have stayed with me while I put the sticker on the tag? Would my children's pediatrician never have asked me about having the same father for my children? Would the attending midwife have explained every step of the process?

In my naiveté, I never gave much thought to how race, class, and gender affected maternal care. I just assumed that women had babies and came home with them. At the time, I would have never thought the maternal mortality rate for America would be the highest among "developed" countries with 26.4 deaths per 100,000 live births.[1] Countries like the U.K. (9.2); Portugal (9); Germany (9); France (7.8); Canada (7.3); Netherlands (6.7); Spain (5.6); Australia (5.5); Ireland (4.7); Sweden (4.4); Italy (4.2), Denmark (4.2); and Finland (3.8) all have rates below 9.2 per 100,000 live births.[2] Over the last six years, I have retold these anecdotes to friends, colleagues, and conference audiences only to find out that I was not alone.Other Black mothers were experiencing the same thing. My story is not unlike other birth trauma stories I started to uncover as I searched for a support group. Because of this research I realized that my story could have ended like Kyria Dixon Johnson's journey. Johnson suffered from internal bleeding after having a scheduled C-section.[3] Ten hours after her surgery Kyria was taken back into surgery where doctors found 3 liters of blood in her abdomen. Unfortunately, they were unable to save her.[4] Had the Cedars Sinai medical staff taken immediate action when Kyria's blood pressure dropped or when her heart began racing and she complained of pain in her abdomen, Kyria would have stood a better chance of surviving. Johnson's husband said he pleaded repeatedly for action, and lawsuit documentation reveals that CT scans were ordered but never performed.[5] Unfortunately, Kyria's story is the rule and not the exception when discussing Black[6] maternal health.

Catherine Pearson's article *Black Women Face More Trauma During Childbirth* highlights the traumatic and sometimes tragic experiences of Black mothers. For example, Tai Haden-Moore had an emergency C-section when she suffered from a placenta abruption. Haden-Moore kept telling doctors that something did not feel right, but she did not know how to fully articulate what she was feeling—other than her stomach felt heavier than normal. Doctors kept telling her that everything was fine because the contraction monitor did not reveal any problems. In this case the doctors did not trust Harden-Moore's instinct that something was amiss.[7] It took Harden-Moore using the bathroom and blood gushing everywhere to get the medical attention she needed. Harden-Moore, when discussing her experience, acknowledged that nobody said anything racist to her, but she felt like her treatment was because she was Black.[8] She stated, "I feel like they always diminish us and think that we're complaining too much, or asking too many questions, or we're drug-seeking . . . those types of things."[9] Harden-Moore is not alone in her opinion regarding the medical establishment. Kiana Shaw was in labor for 52 hours before having a C-section. During 12 of those hours, she waited without medication for a bed to become available in the labor and delivery wing of the hospital, all while experiencing contractions. When she was finally given pain medication, the medicine temporarily blinded her and made her lose the ability to talk. In addition to the lack of pain medication and explanation of what was given to her, when she informed hospital staff that she was going to breastfeed, they gave her daughter formula anyway. As a first-time mother, she did not know what to expect, and like me, much of the process was not explained to her. Shaw felt that her birth trauma contributed to her postpartum depression.

Annette Brookins delivered her daughter stillborn at 39 weeks and 5 days because of a knot in the baby's umbilical cord.[10] When discussing the delivery options for her daughter, Brookins recalled the physician saying, "We can use the suction machine. It's not like she'll feel it—and kind of snickered."[11] The doctor was referring to the stillborn baby's ability to feel the tug of being led through the birth canal with the machine. The emotional toll of delivering a child that she would not take home coupled with the doctor's insensitive comments prompted Brookins's feelings about the need for culturally sensitive physicians. Brookins stated, "I would like for [care providers] to be culturally sensitive to the black female experience and to recognize and check their own biases. I want them to treat us with the same care and concern that they show white women and children."[12]

When I started researching this topic, I found article after article and study after study discussing the health disparities facing Black mothers. The Center for Reproductive Rights reports that "black women in the United States are between three and four times more likely to die from pregnancy related causes than white women and twice as likely to suffer from severe maternal morbidity."[13] Severe maternal morbidity "refers to instances where women almost die from a life-threatening complication during pregnancy or childbirth."[14] The most common pregnancy related complications that may lead to death if not treated in a timely manner include: severe bleeding, blood clots (embolism), pregnancy induced high blood pressure (preeclampsia) and stroke (cerebrovascular accident).

Two decades ago, infant mortality became a research topic. With the technological advances surrounding ultrasound and amniocentesis testing, more emphasis was placed on women delivering healthy babies rather than the needs of women. Women were seen as baby carriers to be managed instead of patients with their own medical needs.[15] Regarding African American women, researchers believed that the high rate of infant mortality could be attributed to the choices of poor, less educated Black women. It was assumed they were not taking care of themselves or their newborn.[16] Researchers are finally looking at maternal health with a critical eye and trying to shift the discussion. In the last 10 years, there has been an increased interest in maternal health, and now, a spotlight is being shined on the challenges that Black mothers face. At the time of this writing Congresswomen Alma Adams and Lauren Underwood created the Black Maternal Caucus. The purpose of the caucus is to "raise awareness within in Congress to establish Black maternal health as a national priority, and explore and advocate for effective, evidence-based, culturally-competent policies and best practices for health outcomes for Black mothers."[17] They have joined forces with Black health care professionals who are committed to highlighting the disparities Black mothers face.

There is a growing body of qualitative research focused on the life or death decisions affecting Black women's pregnancy, labor, birth, and postpartum care. NPR and ProRepublica, in a joint endeavor, collected over 200 stories from African American mothers across the country who shared their birth experiences. Overwhelmingly, Black mothers reported being devalued, disrespected, and treated with contempt.[18] In a 2019 survey of 212 Black mothers, Harper reported that 77.89 percent of respondents felt that African-American mothers do not receive the same level of care as White mothers when dealing with labor and delivery staff. In the same study 22.11 percent said yes, Black mothers received the same level of care.[19] It is interesting to note that some mothers felt they were treated well because they had private insurance—which is an issue of class. For a full list of the survey responses see appendix A. "Black women told of medical providers who equated being African American with being poor, uneducated, noncompliant, and unworthy."[20] In a country where addressing systemic racism and bias affects many industries, the medical field is no different. The nursing culture, specifically that of labor and delivery, is rooted in a White, middle-class female experience which does not make room for the challenges that Black mothers face.[21]

A White nursing culture, unconscious bias, and systemic racism within the medical system has given way to the under treatment of pain in Black patients. Harden-Moore's request for pain medication exemplifies an incorrect belief about African Americans and pain management. A 2016 study conducted by the University of Virginia found that White medical students and residents "had 'fantastical' biological fallacies about racial differences in patients."[22] Medical professionals from that study reported believing that Black skin was thicker than White skin, that Black blood coagulated faster, and that the nerve endings of Blacks were less sensitive than Whites.[23] These incorrect assumptions can be attributed to the unconscious bias and stereotypes that have been circulated about African Americans for centuries. While many of these stories discuss specific complications that were left unattended to by medical staff, there is also this assumption that only poor, less educated African American women face these kinds of challenges, yet research shows that class and education do not change the outcome for Black mothers. A 2016 analysis of five years of data found that Black, college-educated mothers who gave birth in local hospitals were more likely to suffer severe complications of pregnancy or childbirth than White women who never graduated from high school.[24]

Nina Martin and Rene Montagne's investigative piece for NPR's *All Things Considered* substantiated this with the story of Shalon Irving a 36-year-old epidemiologist working at the Centers for Disease Control (CDC). Irving died of complications due to hypertension three weeks after giving birth to her first and only child, Soleil Irving. One would think that with Shalon Irving's education (PhD) and health insurance, her circumstances would have been different. Even tennis star Serena Williams dealt with birth trauma. Williams had a C-section and when she became short of breath, she became worried. Because of her history and knowledge of pulmonary embolisms (blood clots), Williams demanded a CT scan and IV heparin drip, and it was revealed that she had multiple blood clots in her lungs. She also broke her C-section stiches from the coughing spells caused by the clots. What Shalon Irvin, Serena Williams and the stories of other Black mothers demonstrate is that Black women, regardless of education or class, are not exempt from the dangers of receiving poor maternal healthcare.

I maintain this bias comes from historical stereotypes that taught Whites how to view the Black body. These stereotypes set in motion the ability for Americans to use the Black body as a blank canvas.[25] During the antebellum period, Black bodies were characterized as strong and capable of extreme physical endurance; hence, the justification for the poor treatment of slaves; the Black body was a thing to be managed, owned, and sold. When Black bodies were described as strong and capable of servitude, they were property. Yet, after slavery ended, the narrative changed, and Black bodies became weak, susceptible to illness and full of imperfections.[26] These historical connections have a direct correlation to the bias that medical professionals carry with them into office visits.

My experiences coupled with my academic interests in cultural discourse, rhetoric (specifically ethos) and document design made me think critically about Black maternal health and how Black mothers are represented in the media. I want to know if the negative discourse and, more importantly, visual representations in conjunction with the ethos of Black women affected the medical establishment's treatment of Black mothers and children. I am curious about the design and content choices made by publishers and authors who create mainstream pregnancy literature. Next, I began to think about all the Internet searches I engaged in as a mom and how many times negativity was associated with Black mothers both in the media (movies, television, and magazines) and the online environment. For the first time, I realized with clarity that my race, class, and gender intersected with my role as a mother and thus began my search in understanding why Black mothers are suffering from so many medical complications during pregnancy, labor, birth, and postpartum care.

As a Technical and Professional Communication (TPC) educator who believes in using technical communication to redress issues of social justice, I wanted to better understand the role technical communication plays in supporting cultural discourses that allowed women to die—particularly in America, one of the richest and most powerful countries in the world. My interest in Black maternal health and TPC answers the call of other TPC scholars who are advocating for the inclusion of topics such as race, culture, gender, and class in pedagogical discussions. If one thinks of the human body as a highly sophisticated, living technology that requires explanation then it is easy to understand why there are so many books, pamphlets, videos, blogs, website and online communities dedicated to childbirth. On first blush, it might seem strange to think of pregnancy literature as technical and professional communication (TPC), but on closer inspection the information is highly technical in many ways. If I am brutally honest with myself and you the reader, it has been my personal experience, that a few TPC scholars, which I have documented in writing, did not see the value in this research and counted it as anecdotal rather than scholarship. I believe that part of the reason why some might not understand this conversation as relevant to TPC is because it is tied to the experiences of women. And we know that society typically places very little value on the experiences of women and even less on the experiences of Black women. It is medical writing and produced and delivered to audiences via written documents and a variety of platforms.

There is a growing body of research situated in technical and professional communication and medical rhetoric that focuses on motherhood, but serious consideration needs to be given to the power of ethos and its ability to affect a medical professional's treatment of patients. TPC scholars such as Britton 1975; Moore 1996, 1997; Pearsall 1975; and Pearsall and Cook 2010 have always engaged in the conversation about neutrality in the field and value is placed on neutrality and objectivity, but it is the application of these values that muddies the waters. We have to start looking at the problem from a perspective that is inclusive of the power of racism in society and to understand that "technical communication is not neutral or objective. Instead, technical communication is political and imbued with values."[27] Lorde (1977), hooks (1989), Morrison, (1992) Roberts (1997), Solinger (2005), Washington (2006), Lay (2000), Koerber (2013), Buchanan (2013), Siegel (2014), Owens (2015), and Collins (1991, 2004) have all contributed to the ongoing conversation about the praxis and rhetoric of motherhood. They come from divergent fields, but all suggest that maternal health is an interdisciplinary field that continues to develop. I enter this conversation by examining ethos of Black mothers as a way to understand how biases affect the standard of maternal care they receive.

If medical professionals are finally admitting that Black mothers are treated differently and that the problem is not necessarily rooted in risk factors but racism, we need to ask why. Dr. Joia Crear-Perry makes the case that race/ethnic background should not be categorized as risk-factors. Dr. Crear-Perry has advocated that health professionals and the media "stop saying and teaching that being black is a risk factor for illness and death. . . . Instead, we need to start telling the truth: It's exposure to racism that is the risk factor."[28] Dr. Crear-Perry argued that when the medical establishment focuses on Blackness as a risk factor, emphasis is placed on the wrong thing. Being Black is not the risk factor, rather racist policies are and Dr. Perry is pushing for a better understanding of risk factors when she stated,

> According to the World Health Organization, a risk factor is any characteristic or exposure that increases an individual's likelihood of developing a disease or injury. Based on well-established data, risk factors are categorized as modifiable or nonmodifiable, and health-care providers use them to counsel patients on how they can avoid or decrease their likelihood of death or disease. Knowing the risk factors allows patients to do things like get tested earlier for an illness, or, for example, participate in a smoking cessation program. Risk factors can include attributes like fair skin for melanoma, which you cannot modify but you can cover or add sunscreen. But no one is saying that whiteness is a risk factor for melanoma. (p. 3)

Dr. Crear-Perry's argument speaks to what other professionals are now saying—something is amiss when it comes to Black maternal health. Former labor and delivery nurse Hakima Payne experienced first-hand the bias that permeates the medical system. As a nurse, she was privy to "victim blaming" conversations and preconceived ideas about women of color. "If those people would only do blah, blah, blah, things would be different."[29] Carrie Murphy's work as a doula places her in a unique position, and she, as a White woman, has noticed that women of color are missing in the birth discussion.

Murphy's blog entry "*According to Pregnancy Books, Only White Women Get Pregnant*" on Mommyish.com is a testament to the image of motherhood in American society. She stated, "I don't know if you've noticed, but women of color are seriously missing from the imagery of anything that has to do with being pregnant, giving birth to a child, or parenting a newborn."[30] Simply put, Black motherhood is not viewed with the same privilege, positive imagery, and narrative as White motherhood. Murphy's sentiment rings true and is hard to overlook when discussing existing pregnancy literature or images in the media. I define pregnancy literature as books created by mainstream authors that are sold in bookstores and online retailers. I am not referring to the handouts, pamphlets and other materials that healthcare providers give to women during and after pregnancy.

I build on the existing scholarship and specifically Dr. Crear-Perry's call to critically understand the effects of racism. My research begs the question—that if Black mothers do not exist for the mainstream public, then do they have any agency when it comes to their needs as women and mothers? In this research, I interrogate the ethos and agency of Black mothers. My primary concern lies with the rhetoric that surrounds motherhood and Black motherhood in American society. I ask the questions:

1. What is the ethos of Black motherhood and how does it stigmatize Black communities and hinder access to safe and effective maternal healthcare?

2. Visually, what does motherhood look like in commercially produced books and how do those images reinforce certain ideologies and principles in American society?

3. How have Black mothers established a space where they advocate for their needs as women and mothers?

I have two sections that work to answer these questions and I foreground the experiences of Black women and mothers in America. Section one is a historical account of Black women's reproductive health and ethos. It includes chapters 1, 2, 3, and 4. In chapter 1, I start with an examination of White womanhood and the historical representations of Black womanhood. I emphasize the nature of motherhood within the context of chattel slavery. I discuss the romanticized image of the White southern woman. I discuss the power within a patriarchal and paternalistic society run by White men. Next, I discuss what motherhood looked like for enslaved women by addressing the challenges they faced and how they reclaimed their agency amid having none. In chapter 2, I discuss the medical culture of the enslaved south, because it helps to understand the tone that was set for dealing with Black women's bodies. In chapter 3, I explore the legislative decisions created to govern Black women's bodies and wombs. As part of my conversation, I discuss how the images of the mammy, breeder, matriarch, welfare queen, crack addicted mother, and teen mom were made to control Black women's reproductive abilities and sexuality. I start with the laws associated with the eugenics movement, and next, I explore the laws associated with birth control and compulsory sterilization. In chapter 4, I return to the topic of ethos, but with a discussion of American ideology, the ideology and ethos of motherhood, and the rhetoric of silence and invisibility. Section two includes chapters 5, 6, 7, and 8 and in this section I explore reproductive health, justice and activism by looking at the work of doulas, grassroots and government agencies, and individual women who are working to change maternal health outcomes for Black mothers. Chapter 5 is a critical discourse analysis of popular pregnancy literature. The goals of the study are to (1) explore how images of motherhood are presented to the public and (2) understand how those images reinforce certain ideologies in society. Chapter 6 is a discussion of how Black women deal with the challenges associated with abortion services. Chapter 7 focuses on the trials Black women face as they seek to have children under the conditions they choose. My discussion looks at the tensions that exist between medically assisted deliveries versus midwife assisted deliveries. In chapter 8 I talk about the work of resistance in raising Black children in American society by discussing the school-to-prison pipeline and the over policing of Black communities.

When I set out to write this book, I envisioned that I would only talk about rhetoric—specifically ethos. However, as I began to unpack this topic, I realized this discussion is applicable to a number of disciplines. As such, this book is for the scholar of rhetoric who is interested in ethos and the rhetoric(s) of silence and listening. It is for the scholar interested in places of topoi and how motherhood is rhetorically used in American culture. This book is for the critical discourse analysis scholar whose interest is primarily the choices of pregnancy book publishers who design for a specific audience. This book is also for the medical professional who wants to understand the silent ways implicit bias is reinforced as well as scholars in the emerging field of rhetorics of health and medicine. Finally, this book is for those individuals who are reproductive justice activists because it explores the intersectionality of Black women's mothering. Finally, I hope this book will help further discussions about the power of ethos and the image of Black maternal health—since White women are not the only women who become pregnant.

NOTES

1. Nina Martin and Renee Montagne, "Black Mothers Keep Dying After Giving Birth, Shalon Irving's Story Explains Why." *National Public Radio*, December 7, 2017, https://www.npr.org/2017/12/07/568948782/black-mothers-keep-dying-after-giving-birth-shalon-irvings-story-explains-why.
2. Martin and Montagne, "Black Mothers Keep Dying."
3. Patrice Cullors, "#Justice4Kyira Means Justice for Black Mothers Everywhere," The Root, June 22, 2017, https://www.theroot.com/justice4kyira-means-justice-for-black-mothers-everywhe-1796340568.
4. Glenda Hatchett, "Judge Hatchett in Her Own Legal Battle After Daughter-in-Law Dies Shortly After Giving Birth," interviewed by Jim Moret, *Inside Edition*, May 16, 2017.
5. Hatchett, *Inside Edition*.
6. I define Black Americans as the ancestors of enslaved Africans who were brought to the United States, and I use terms Black and African American interchangeably. However, I am clear that some people who identify as Black do not consider themselves African American or the descendants of enslaved Africans brought to America.
7. Kimberly Harper, "Implicit Bias, Visual Rhetoric, and Black Maternal Health: Understanding the Real Risk Factor" in *From Band-Aids to Scalpels: Motherhood Experiences in/of Medicine* eds. Rohini Bannerjee and Karim Mukhida (Ontario: Demeter Press, April 2021).
8. Catherine Pearson, "Black Women Face More Trauma During Childbirth," *Huffpost*, June 18, 2018, https://www.huffpost.com/entry/black-women-childbirth-mortality-trauma_n_5b045eaae4b0784cd2af0f71.
9. Pearson, "Black Women," 3.
10. Pearson, "Black Women," 6.
11. Pearson, "Black Women," 6.
12. Pearson, "Black Women," 6.
13. Center for Reproductive Rights. *Research Overview of Maternal Mortality and Morbidity in the United States*. New York: Center for Reproductive Rights, 2016, 1.
14. Center, "Research," 1.
15. Marika Seigel, *The Rhetoric of Pregnancy* (Chicago: The University of Chicago Press, 2014), x.
16. Linda Villarosa, "Why America's Black Mothers and Babies Are in a Life-or-Death Crisis," *New York Times*, April 11, 2018. https://www.nytimes.com/2018/04/11/magazine/black-mothers-babies-death-maternal-mortality.html.
17. Alma Adams, "Congresswomen Adams and Underwood Launch Black Maternal Health Caucus," Congresswoman Alma Adams website, April 19, 2019, https://adams.house.gov/media-center/press-releases/congresswomen-adams-and-underwood-launch-black-maternal-health-caucus.
18. Martin and Montagne, "Black Mothers Keep Dying."
19. Kimberly Harper. "Only White Women Get Pregnant Survey," April–May 2019.
20. Martin and Montagne, "Black Mothers Keep Dying."
21. Martin and Montagne, "Black Mothers Keep Dying."
22. Linda Villarosa, "Why America's Black Mothers and Babies Are in a Life-or-Death Crisis," *New York Times*, April 11, 2018. https://www.nytimes.com/2018/04/11/magazine/black-mothers-babies-death-maternal-mortality.html. Accessed July 03, 2018.
23. Villarosa, "Why America's Black Mothers."
24. Martin and Montagne, "Black Mothers Keep Dying."
25. Patricia Hill Collins, *Black Sexual Politics: African American, Gender, and the New Racism* (New York: Routledge, 2004).
26. Martin and Montagne, "Black Mothers Keep Dying."
27. Natasha Jones, "The Technical Communicator as Advocate: Integrating a SocialJustice Approach in Technical Communcation," *Journal of Technical Writing and Communication*, 46 no. 3, (2016): 342–361, 345.

28. Joia Crear-Perry, "Race Isn't a Risk Factor in Maternal Health. Racism Is." *Rewire News*, April 11 2018, https://rewire.news/article/2018/04/11/maternal-health-replace-race-with-racism/, 2.
29. Martin and Montagne, "Black Mothers Keep Dying."
30. Carrie Murphy, "According to Pregnancy Books, Only White Women Get Pregnant," Mommyish.com, January 24, 2014, https://www.mommyish.com/women-of-color-childbirth/, para. 2, Accessed October 1, 2016.

Chapter One

Historical Representations of Black Motherhood

Black women have a long history of displacement and loss of agency due to chattel slavery, the eugenics movement, and Jim Crow. Unfortunately, the demonizing images that grew out of those circumstances affected the way Black motherhood was constructed for public consumption. This misrepresentation can be attributed to the historical images of Black women and the space(s) they have traditionally occupied for White America's infrastructures. Patrician Hill Collins asserts that these institutions (schools, media, and government entities, and businesses) reproduce and transmit ideologies that paint Black women as a negative *other*.[1] In this chapter I explore the historical representations of White and Black womanhood. I discuss how White patriarchy, paternalism, and violence crafted a unique power relationship between White women and the slaves they owned. Finally, I discuss the agency of enslaved Black mothers and free Black women in the North.

WHITE WOMANHOOD'S INFLUENCE ON BLACK WOMANHOOD

Black womanhood, historically, has been defined as an anomaly or aberration to White men's gender expectations for White women. In the early nineteenth-century White women were defined by what researchers coined as the "cult of true womanhood." The qualities associated with true womanhood included "four cardinal virtues—piety, purity, submissiveness and domesticity."[2] American society catered to these standards by creating a social structure that provided wealthy White women with the time and means to manage their homes rather than participate in the physical labor of housework. Thus, enslaved women's labor included cooking, cleaning, and child rearing which also included wet nursing White children. With her time free to focus on raising moral children and religious activities, the *virtuous White woman* became the symbol of American womanhood and eventually motherhood. Historians furthered these stereotypes when they romanticized accounts of plantation life in southern literature that supported a proslavery discourse. These stories painted one picture for public consumption but neglected to discuss the struggle White women faced living under the restrictions of White male patriarchy, nor did these books highlight the power they held within the paternalistic system of chattel slavery or the violence they inflicted on enslaved persons.

In American society, particularly the antebellum south, men held the power of life and death for the slaves they owned. And they held the power to *create* and *enforce* their vision of womanhood on White and Black women. While all women were objectified, White women were stereotyped as helpless, domestic, submissive, and emotional and thought of as inferior to White men, thus in need of protection and guidance. Under the restraints of White patriarchy Black women were stereotyped as anti-feminine, hypersexual, and animalistic. These stereotypes created a proslavery discourse that placed the White woman's sexuality, motherhood, and sense of self on a pedestal to be protected and cherished by White men as they denigrated and sexually assaulted Black women. White women had to be protected from Black men—usually with violence as seen in the 1915 movie *Birth of a Nation*.

Despite the narrative of the asexual, nonthreatening, and docile Uncle Tom, Black men were still seen as a threat to White women's sexuality and White patriarchy. Dorothy Giddings's research suggests, as do I, that Black men's mythical sexual appetite for White women was used as a justification for violence under the system of chattel slavery; and when freedom came this narrative was, then, used to justify violence and economic sanctions enacted upon newly freed Black families. It was widely thought that without the restraint of slavery, free Black men would lay in wait for White women. Giddings refers to Philip Bruce, a Harvard graduate and historian who advanced this assumption in his work *The Plantation Negro as a Freeman*. Bruce suggested free Blacks who were no longer under the control of White superiority would regress to a criminal and barbaric nature.[3] Bruce went on to say, "Black men found something strangely alluring and seductive in the appearance of white women."[4] Periodicals like *Harper's Weekly* furthered Bruce's damaging narrative about Black men when they described them as losing the proper amount of respect for White women. This myth became rooted in America's national discourse regarding contact between Black men and White women and spread into anti-Black sentiment.

The anti-Black sentiment that spread across the country prior to the secession of the southern states in late 1860 and early 1861 and after the Civil War was evident with President Lincoln and later President Andrew Johnson. While running for election to the Illinois senate Lincoln engaged in a debate with incumbent senator Stephen Douglas. When the debate turned to slavery which was what their seven debates were about President Lincoln was quoted as saying,

> I am not, nor have even been, in favor of bringing about in any way the social and political equality of the white and black races,—that I am not nor ever have been in favor of making voters or jurors of negroes, nor of qualifying them to hold office, nor to intermarry with white people; and I will say in addition to this that there is a physical difference between the white and black races which I believe will forever forbid the two races living together on terms of social and political equality.[5]

Although Lincoln freed enslaved people with the 1863 Emancipation Proclamation, his act did little to change the racial and political climate of America. Lincoln's successor, President Johnson, was not concerned with the wellbeing of newly free men and women; rather, he was more interested in oppressing them. He was quoted as saying, "This is . . . a country for white men, and by God, as long as I am President, it shall be a government for white men."[6] In addition to presidential leadership, state laws across the country were full of racist polices that prevented Black Americans from fully participating in American life.[7] Consequently, the written law coupled with cultural opinion furthered a negative discourse about Black Americans. Government officials, national periodicals, and historians were all responsible for circulating dangerous assumptions about Black Americans—assumptions that would eventually become cemented in the pathos of southern race relations.

Chattel slavery depended on a paternalistic power structure that was full of violence and death. Patriarchy gave White men an obscene amount of control over the lives of women. White men, particularly those of the planter class aristocracy, went to great lengths to control White women's sexuality. For example, White women were not allowed to travel without a male chaperone and spousal abuse was considered a right of the husband. If a White woman was caught having a sexual relationship with a slave which resulted in a pregnancy, her husband, father, or other male relative could sell or kill the child.[8] These restrictions, along with the idea that White women needed protection, trapped White women in a vacuum where they were powerless under the authority of White male patriarchy; however, within this gilded cage she still had a considerable amount of power over the slaves she owned. Because the White woman has been romanticized in history as caregiver for all people the depth of her power over slaves is often downplayed or not discussed at all.

Southern literature and movies like *Gone with the Wind* reminisce about the genteel nature of southern mistresses. Despite the paternalism and violence of chattel slavery they were stereotyped as being the "softer female head of the household" who "gently ran the household and nurtured their families, black and white" who had "concern for the plight of other women, slaves among them."[9] However, slave narratives tell a different story about the violence enslaved men and women received at the hands of White mistresses. These contested sights of memory dispel the image of a happy slave and the firm, but fair plantation mistress. In Norman Yetman's edited collection *When I was a Slave: Memoirs from the Slave Narrative Collection*, former enslaved women recall the meanness of their mistresses in the excerpts below:

Julia Brown—
"She'd lash us with a cowhide whip."[10]

Fannie Moore—
"She whip me many times with a cowhide, till I was black and blue."[11]

Harriet Robinson—
"Master Sam did not never whip me, but Miss Julia whipped me everyday in the morning. During the War she beat us so terrible . . . Miss Julia would take me by my ears and but my head against the wall."[12]

Frederic Douglass—
"She used to sit in a large rocking chair near the middle of the room, with a heavy cowskin . . . and I speak within the truth when I say, that those girls seldom passed that chair, during the day, without a blow from that cowskin, either upon their bare arms or upon their shoulders. As they passed her she would draw that cowskin and give them a blow, saying, '*move faster, you black jip!*' and again, '*take that, you black jip!*' continuing, *if you don't move faster, I will give you more.*' The lady would go on, singing her sweet hymns, as though her righteous soul were signing for the holy realms of paradise."[13]

These narratives expose the violence slaves received from the hands of their White mistresses.

Just as slaves had to calculate their interactions with slave masters and overseers, deference was also needed to shield themselves from the fury of White mistresses, who were dealing with their own sense of powerlessness, shame from extramarital affairs of their husbands or sons with female slaves, and shame from the children born of those sexual interactions.

In *Out of the House of Bondage* Thavolia Glymph refutes the romanticized notion of the White mistress when she states, "contrary to most interpretations, violence on the part of white women was integral to the making of slavery, crucial to shaping black and white women's understanding of what it meant to be female, and not more defensible than masters' violence."[14] Ultimately, the cult of womanhood and chattel slavery supported a White supremacist system that used race and gender to exploit women. These stereotypes justified the brutal treatment of Black bodies—including Black women who bore the burden of physical labor on plantation fields, unwanted sexual encounters with slave owners, violence from slave mistresses, and the responsibility of birthing and raising children that would be sold.

Of importance to proslavery discourse and the image of White womanhood are the concepts of religiosity and piety. Pious and pure White women did not behave in ways that would raise questions about their morality or sexual desires. Alternatively, Black women could not claim piety and purity as virtues because they supposedly welcomed all sexual encounters. According to proslavery discourse Black women would readily have sex with any Black man and sought to seduce the White men they encountered. Additionally, Black mothers who were "breeder women" were thought to lack maternal feelings because they were chattel—therefore, lacking the basic emotions associated with humanity. Black mothers from the antebellum period fell into two categories. The first category is that of enslaved mothers who lacked autonomy over the emotions and bodies of themselves and their children. The second category is that of free Negro women in the North who struggled to control what motherhood meant in the context of antebellum freedom.

Enslaved Mothers

Chattel slavery was problematic for both White and Black women, but it had damning consequences for Black mothers and children. Black women's status as chattel laid the groundwork for an archetype of Black woman that was antithetical to the virtues of motherhood. Chattel slavery dehumanized enslaved mothers and controlled their emotional expressions and agency. Under the system of chattel slavery, Black mothers were not considered women; therefore, it was thought they were unable to demonstrate the same virtues of nurture and emotional care that White women extended to their families. The irony is that these same women were responsible for raising White children. Out of the proslavery discourse of the time grew a stereotype that removed Black mothers from the expression of emotion.[15] However, to the contrary, Black mothers expressed their sense of care and nurture in two significant ways: transmitting acquired immunities to their children and mourning.

In his book *Know Thy Self*, psychologist Dr. Na'im Akbar discusses the responsibility each generation bears in preparing the next generation for success. The point that is applicable to enslaved motherhood is Akbar's concept of "transmitting acquired immunities."[16] Akbar defines this as the community's and or parent's responsibility to teach children the ways of self-protection from the social and physical diseases of society. In the context of chattel slavery, this meant enslaved mothers had to prepare their children for the emotional stress of family separation, back-breaking work, and physical violence at the whims of slaveholders. For women in particular they had to prepare their daughters for sexual violence at the hands of slave owners and overseers. Enslaved mothers and children lived in a perpetual limbo—always awaiting the possibility that they might be sold away from each other. Slave narratives are full of stories about children being sold away from their mothers. Former enslaved woman Julia Brown's recollection is heartbreaking. She recalled, "Oh! It was pitiful to see children taken from their mothers' breasts, mothers sold, husbands sold from wives."[17]

Furthermore, Delia Garlic's traumatic experience of never seeing her mother again affected her tremendously. She was the youngest of thirteen children, but she only knew one of her siblings. Her family was split up well before her birth. After being beaten by her owners, she ran away from the big house and back to her mother's cabin in the slave quarters in the middle of the night. Garlic was taken from Richmond that very night and sold away from her mother. She never saw her again. So many families were displaced because of slave auctions. Fannie Moore from Asheville, NC, remembered how breeder women and their children would be put on display at slave auctions. She recalled the fear and anguish of the slaves when word spread that a speculator was on the plantation.

> When de speculator come all de slave start a-shakin'. No one know who is a-goin'. Den sometimes dey take'em and sell'em on de block. De "breed woman" always bring more money den de rest, even de men. When dey put her on de block dey put all her children around her to show folks how fast she can have chillen. When she sold, her family never see her again. She never know how many chillen she have. Sometimes she have colored chillen and sometimes White. Tain't no use to say anything, cause if she do she just get whipped.[18]

In an attempt to prepare their children for the perils of slavery enslaved mothers relied heavily on their faith in God to help them and their families deal with the brutality and the psychological stress of losing their children. And, they taught their children the same thing—rely on God, thus transmitting acquired immunities to their families. Delia Garlic's experience also provided evidence of faith in God. Garlic recalled the last interaction she had with her mother before being sold. "I has thought so many time through all dese years how Mammy looked dat night. She pressed my hand in both of her and said: 'Be good and trust in de lord.'"[19] Garlic carried that advice with her as she was sold two more times before freedom came. Garlic said of her faith, "Trustin' in de lord was de only hope of de poor black ciritters in dem days. Us just prayed for strength to endure it to de end. We did not 'spect nothing' but to stay in bondage till we died."[20]

In her recent work, C. L. Webster has offered further evidence of this transmission of acquired immunities in her discussion of Sojourner Truth's narrative and the coping skills Truth learned from her mother. Webster wrote:

> In her narrative, Truth described other mechanisms for coping with the ambiguous future passed down to her by her mother. The religious education Truth received from her mother, Mau-mau Bett, attempted to prepare herself for moments of trauma and loss by surrendering life to God. In the occasional undisturbed time Truth's mother possessed with her children, she would, "endeavor to show [her children] their Heavenly Father, as the only being who could protect them in their perilous condition." Her mother had anticipated and accepted her imminent sale away from her children and thus relinquished her fate and authority over her children to a higher power. In doing so, Mau-mau Bett, like other enslaved women, attempted to prepare her children for the inevitability of disruptive events.[21]

These actions gave enslaved mothers a form of control as they attempted to pass on the importance of deference as a protection against violence and faith in God to their children. For enslaved mothers the natural expression of care and concern that mothers have for their children was controlled by a system that dehumanized her and her children. She was denied autonomy over the care of her children and made to experience the unthinkable—having her children sold. To reclaim some control, enslaved mothers used the process of mourning to express the maternal emotions that were often denied them.

Mourning was a way of reclaiming a sense of power and control over the lives of their children. In addition to mourning children who were sold away, enslaved mothers also mourned the physical death of children who died shortly after childbirth. According to birth and death records, "almost half of all enslaved children died within the first two weeks of birth and another quarter died by age two."[22] Fannie Moore, in her memoir, told of the extreme grief her mother felt when her brother George died. "My mammy grieve lots over brother George, who die with de fever. . . . Poor Mammy she kneel by de bed an cry her eyes out. Old Uncle Allen, he make pine box for him and carry him to de grave yard over de hill. My Mammy just plow and cry as she watch 'em put George in de ground."[23] The inability of Moore's mother to care for her sick child and then his death and burial demonstrate the loss of agency that enslaved mothers had over their children—even if they were sick. Her desire to care for her child was thwarted. Her desire to bury him was precluded. The psychological trauma of being separated from each other, along with the severing of the mother-child bond laid the foundation for the proslavery narrative that Black mothers did not care for their children. Slave narratives recount the distress enslaved mothers experienced, but another side to the discussion deals with free Black women in the North who also struggled with the negative perceptions of Black motherhood.

Free Black Mothers in the North

Northern freedwomen, while able to have access to their children (depending on the circumstances of their own freedom), still dealt with the challenges of a proslavery discourse about motherhood. To combat the negative discourse, free Black publications used their power to produce a counter narrative that showcased Black mothers as pillars of the family. Publications like the *Christian Recorder* reimagined Black motherhood as embodying the ideals of Christian morality, domesticity, and the notion that mothers held the power to "guide their children to success."[24] Free women of the North faced the challenges of defining motherhood for themselves. Part of the rhetoric that grew out of their pursuit of agency and power is the narrative of racial uplift. Many free women and later Black women of middle-class standing saw racial uplift as part of the job of Black mothers.

As the institution of slavery in America developed and was eventually abolished, the need to dominate Black women's sexuality was necessary for White patriarchy's continued existence. Consequently, Black women emerged from chattel slavery, Reconstruction, Jim Crow, and the Civil Rights movement carrying the burden of being stereotyped as either a mammy, breeder woman, matriarch, unwed welfare queen, or Jezebel.[25] Out of chattel slavery grew a way in which Black mothers would come to be seen, written about, and discussed.

Black mothers, according to the prevailing narrative are not loving, supportive, positive, or economically independent of the government. These images, along with the rhetoric that surrounds Black families, make "racism, sexism, and poverty appear to be natural, normal and an inevitable part of everyday life."[26] While Collins' research asserts that these images are used to control and objectify Black women's bodies as an *other*, I add that these images create a powerful ideology and ethos that are fostered in the thinking, discourse, and behaviors of White society and institutions, thereby affecting Black motherhood and the disregard for Black life, which contributes to the high maternal mortality rate in Black communities. This ideology and expression is antithetical to how Black communities understand and experience Black motherhood and such narratives do not reflect the values held by Black mothers or Black people. Fundamental to the oppression of Black women are these images along with the anti-Black narratives that have been attached to Black families.[27] In chapter 2, "Setting the Tone," I discuss the medical culture of the enslaved south as a means for understanding how the disregard for Black life was woven into the fabric of the American experience.

NOTES

1. Patricia Hill Collins, *Black Feminist Thought: Knowledge Consciousness, and the Politics of Empowerment* (New York: Routledge, 1991), 86.
2. Barbara Welter, "The Cult of True Womanhhood:1820–1860," *American Quarterly* 18, no. 2 (1966): 15–174, 152.
3. Paula Giddings, *When and Where I Enter* (New York: Amistad, 2006).
4. Giddings, *When and Where*, 27.
5. Eastern Illinois University, "Bulletin 220—The Lincoln-Douglas Debate at Charleston, IL September 18, 1858" (1957). Eastern Illinois University Bulletin. 60.http://thekeep.eiu.edu/eiu_bulletin/60, 53.
6. Carol Anderson, *White Rage: The Unspoken Truth of Our Racial Divide* (New York: Bloomsbury Publishing, 2017), 18.
7. Anderson, *White Rage*.
8. Thavolia Glympyh, *Out of the House of Bondage: The Transformation of the Plantation Household* (New York: Cambridge University Press, 2008).
9. Glympyh, *Out of the House of Bondage*, 23.
10. Norman R. Yetman, *When I was a Slave: Memoirs from the Slave Narrative Collection* (Mineola: Dover Publications, 2002), "Brown Interview," 20.
11. Yetman, *When I was a Slave*, "Moore Interview," 88.
12. Yetman, *When I was a Slave*, "Robinson Interview," 112.
13. Glympyh, *Out of the House of Bondage*, 35, 23.
14. Glymph, *Out of the House*, 5.
15. Crystal Lynn Webster, "In Pursuit of Autonomous Womanhood: Nineteenth-Century Black Motherhood in the U.S. North." *Slavery & Aboloition* 38, no. 2 (2017): 425–440.
16. Na'im Akbar, *Know thy Self* (Talllahassee: Mind Production and Associates, 1998), 9.
17. Yetman, *When I was a Slave*, 21.
18. Yetman, *When I was a Slave*, 90.
19. Yetman, *When I was a Slave*, 44.
20. Yetman, *When I was a Slave*, 44.
21. Crystal Lynn Webster, "In Pursuit of Autonomous Womanhood: Nineteenth-Century Black Motherhood in the U.S. North." *Slavery & Aboloition* 38, no. 2 (2017): 425–440.
22. Sasha Turner, "The Nameless and the Forgotten: Maternal Grief, Sacred Protection, and the Archive of Slavery." *Slavery & Abolition* 38, no. 2 (2017): 232–250, 232.
23. Yetman, *When I was a Slave*, 91.
24. Webster, "In Pursuit of Autonomous Womanhood," 425–440, 434.
25. Collins, *Black Feminist Thought*.
26. Collins, *Black Feminist Thought*, 68.
27. Collins, *Black Feminist Thought*.

Chapter Two

Setting the Tone

Black women's loss of control over their sexuality and reproductive rights has been a problem ever since their 1526 arrival in South Carolina as part of a Spanish Expedition[1] and some ninety-three years later when enslaved Africans returned to the shores of Jamestown, Virginia in 1619. No matter the date, a key component of chattel slavery was the need to treat Black bodies as an *other* and deny them a sense of humanity and personhood. Slave traders and owners used written, oral, and visual discourse from politics, business, and medical institutions to justify the enslavement of Africans. All these areas worked together, in dehumanizing Black bodies, thus setting the tone for how White Americans would come to understand enslaved persons and their bodies for generations to come.

For chattel slavery to thrive as a culture, people needed an ideology and conceptual system of meanings, symbols, and metaphors to influence how community members perceive and experience their environment.[2] People needed to have a common discourse that supported the financial and social goals of chattel slavery, which was monetary.

Collectively these groups inculcated American culture with racist ideologies that trace back to the arrival of English colonists in 1619.[3] Colonists arriving in the *new world* were escaping religious persecution, poor living and working conditions, and sometimes their own indentured servitude. They brought with them their hopes for a better life and an understanding of human classification according to their religious beliefs.The Puritan settlers of New England along with the 1619 settlers who arrived on Virginia's coast already had religious ideas that affirmed their belief in African slavery. Kendi suggests these ideas of African inferiority were two centuries old by the time colonists reached the shores of North America. One of the earliest evidences of written discourse that promoted an anti-Black ideology and a justification for African enslavement is Gomes Eanes de Zurara's book *The Chronicle of the Discovery and Conquest of Guinea*. The book was commissioned by Prince Henry, the nephew of King Alfonso V of Portugal, and is a description of the king's entry into the slave trade.[4] Kendi observes that prior to and during King Alfonso's participation in the slave trade, most of the enslaved were Eastern Europeans who had been captured by the Turkish.[5] Once King Alfonso V became involved, the concept of who could be enslaved changed. In his book, Zurara describes the kings' slave trading activities as a "missionary expedition" and rewrites slavery as a uniquely Black experience.[6] This distinction is important because prior to the Portuguese foray into slave trading and Zurara's book, the concept of what a slave looked like was not explicitly linked to Africans, Black skin, or even a group of people—per se. It is Zurara who distinguished between Black and White skin when he described Black skin as *ugly* and suggests Moors appeared to be visitors from hell.[7] Zurara further suggests that Africans needed to be enslaved because they lacked religious guidance and civil salvation.

By focusing on the history of racist ideologies, Kendi highlights a very important point to consider; the desire to oppress and classify humanity has always been part of the human experience and English settlers were already conditioned to have anti-Black attitudes. I contend that American chattel slavery is based on those anti-Black and pro-slavery sentiments colonizers brought with them when they first arrived in 1526 and again in 1619. Similar to the Portuguese, French, English, and Dutch who colonized the continent of Africa and engaged in the Transatlantic Slave Trade, American pro-slavery advocates used religious justification to sanitize their dirty work. American slaveholders cited Black people as the descendants from the cursed tribe of Ham who were destined to live a life of servitude.

In addition to religious justification, slaveholders also used scientific racism to ensure that enslaved Africans would be a commodity and not a human being. Those using a medical justification for slavery suggested "Black's physical and mental defects made it impossible for them to survive without White supervision and care."[8] They reinforced the idea enslaved Africans were automatically inferior to Whites in every way possible. Black bodies were stereotyped as both sickly and strong, yet always inferior. Medical propaganda was used to rationalize the violent treatment of enslaved people and it was used to ensure a social stratification that kept Blacks at the bottom of America's social order. Dorothy Roberts furthers this when she states, "The social order established by powerful White men was founded on two inseparable core beliefs: the dehumanization of Africans on the basis of race, and the control of women's sexuality and reproduction."[9]

Scholars in the disciplines of rhetoric, linguistics, and critical discourse analysis have written extensively about the power of discourse to create, maintain and reproduce racism. Teun van Dijk emphasizes that the institutions of politics, media, academia, and business control various types of public discourse.[10] And, "they have the largest sake in maintaining white group dominance" and are quite adept as "persuasively formulating their ethnic opinions."[11] Sara Mills suggests that the individual beliefs of a person in a society are derived from "larger-scale belief systems structured by discursive frameworks, which are given credibility and force by imperial power structures."[12] I agree with both van Dijk and Mills in their assessment of languages' ability to control power structure, and I offer that often what seems irrational is made acceptable because of erroneous narratives that are circulated in society as truths. For enslaved Africans the narratives of their inhumanity and incompetence were the basis for their enslavement and served as a reminder that words have power in our cultural systems. As such, the rest of this chapter is about the medical culture of chattel slavery and how it affected motherhood. It is about the images of Black women that were created to serve a White, male powerbase. It is about enslaved women's labor and how it affected their reproductive rights. It is about the ways in which enslaved mothers sought to control their own bodies despite their lot in life. It is about the culture of abuse within chattel slavery and the medical practices and discourse that grew out of America's early beginnings.

THE MEDICAL CULTURE OF ANTEBELLUM SOUTH

The practice of medicine in the antebellum south was full of real and fictitious health conditions, dangerous medical experiments, and violence. Physicians belied the mental and physical woes of Black bodies in widely circulated medical journals and textbooks claiming "the primitive nervous systems of Blacks were 'immune' to physical and emotional pain and to mental illness."[13] To further support these claims prominent physicians like Samuel A. Cartwright used several techniques to *prove* enslaved patients were inferior—one of which was lying. Cartwright published pamphlets and journal articles with fictitious "black" diseases. In her book *Medical Apartheid*, Harriet Washington describes these illnesses:

> By 1851, Cartwright had also discovered and described a host of imaginary "black" diseases, whose principal symptoms seemed to be a lack of enthusiasm for slavery.... Hebetude drapetoania was a condition that caused slaves to run away from insanity. Hebetude was a singular laziness or shiftlessness that caused slaves to mishandle and abuse their owners' property. Dysthesia Aethiopica was another black behavior malady, which was characterized by a desire to destroy the property of White slave owners. Cartwright claimed that it "differs from other species of mental disease, as it is accompanied with *physical signs or lesions of the body* discoverable to the medical observer...."
> Struma Africana was a form of tuberculosis that physicians misdiagnosed as a

peculiarly African disease. Cachexia Africana referred to blacks' supposed propensity for eating nonfood substances such as clay, chalk, and dirt.[14]

Cartwright prescribed corporal punishment, fresh air, and sunshine to remedy the slothful state of enslaved patients.[15]

The research of Cartwright and his peers proved useful in adding to the conceptual system of chattel slavery that was built to promulgate "black biological primitivism and inferiority in every aspect of life."[16] In addition to their written discourse, physicians who treated Blacks were contradictory in their assessments. On the one hand slaves were weak and susceptible to intellectual and physical ailments, but on the other hand they were strong and could withstand brutality and strenuous manual labor. Slaves suffered from sicknesses due to malnutrition, badly constructed slave quarters, extreme physical labor, and psychological and physical abuse rather than made up sicknesses created by southern physicians and scientific racism.

According to slave narratives it was common practice for doctors to use enslaved Blacks in their medical experiments. Blacks' inability to give consent allowed physicians to use their bodies unscrupulously. In addition, if they received treatment—their owner was considered the patient; therefore, the doctor only considered the slaveholder regarding the best course of action. Most antebellum doctors believed that Blacks did not suffer from pain or anxiety. And, because of this belief enslaved patients endured surgeries, bloodletting, blistering, perspiring, trephination (drilling a hole in the scalp), quinine, calomel, arsenic, and mercury treatments meant to induce vomiting and diarrhea and amputations sometimes without anesthesia or concern from doctors about their mental or physical wellbeing.[17] As far as slaveholders were concerned medical experimentation was part of a slave's job responsibilities. For example, Thomas Jefferson used 200 of his slaves as test subjects for a smallpox vaccine before vaccinating his White family.[18] Losing control of their body for medical procedures further exacerbated the loss of agency that slaves faced. Black women did not escape the burden of medical experimentation and dangerous treatments. My own view is that their situation was intensified because slave-owners depended on their wombs for sustaining the enslaved workforce of plantation life, thus having multiple children was part of their work-life responsibilities.

Enslaved women's value was based on their ability to have children; consequently, women who were thought to be barren suffered. Schwartz writes that "young women who had not demonstrated fertility faced the possibility of separation from family as well as additional labor" to compensate for their lack of children.[19] Barren women were considered a liability because they did not add to the workforce and were often sold. Infertility was such a concern that enslaved women were subjected to physical exams where they were stripped naked and physicians would conduct a vaginal exam to verify if she had already given birth or looked healthy enough to give birth. Slaveholders viewed fertility and menstruation as part of plantation management and employed antebellum physicians to help with the process. However, most physicians of the time lacked a clear understanding of fertility, menstruation, and birth control which made the uncertainty of conceiving and successfully giving birth an added stress for enslaved women.

Fertility and Menstruation

The culture of chattel slavery was not set up to treat enslaved mothers like women or patients, and by 1852 physicians still struggled with pinning down the age of onset for a menstrual cycle, normal cycle length and blood loss. Despite medical care from White doctors, Black women depended on each other for contraceptives and maternal healthcare and used a variety of techniques to see a mother through pregnancy, labor, and postpartum care. Enslaved women shared information about birth control and regulating their menstrual cycles with each other. Antebellum maternal health focused on rapid reproduction. As the field of obstetrics became its own specialty, interest in menstruation became a dominant part of the discussion around fertility and was often conflated with issues of fertility, abortion, and birth control.

The wellbeing of the mother and the children she bore was not of great importance, which meant enslaved women were prevented from using birth control. Many doctors did not believe enslaved women had the intelligence to regulate their menstrual cycle and control their own fertility. For example, E. M. Pendleton, a Georgia doctor, found it impossible "for the 'stupid negro' to have discovered a reliable means to do so, when sober, thinking men had failed for ages to find a means for regulating the menses."[20] However enslaved women did know and they were often successful. Enslaved mothers practiced a form of birth control called spacing as a way to give their bodies time to recover from birth and provide their existing children with better care. Spacing was antithetical to the slaveholder's concept of motherhood, which was to have as many children as fast as possible. Eventually slaveholders and their physicians came to realize cotton plant root and breast feeding were both effective forms of birth control. Slave women would make tea out of the root or chew it while they worked. Cotton root was a perfect solution because it was cheap, accessible, and easy for a woman to hide her use of the herb.[21] Enslaved women also used other natural remedies like dogwood root and dogfennel together to prevent pregnancy; jimsonweed to abort a pregnancy; gunpowder mixed with milk or ingesting pellets of birdshot to prevent conception; and squaw weed or golden ragwort leaves tea to help alleviate menstrual cramps.

As I noted earlier, enslaved mothers used breastfeeding to prevent pregnancy, but this was difficult because slaveholders usually allowed a child to nurse for nine months; however, some research indicated some children nursed until age two. I suggest enslaved women's use of natural remedies to prevent pregnancy along with breast feeding was an act of resistance and a small, yet meaningful, form of agency. These acts of defiance were communal and only shared with a woman once she became a mother. The culture of care that enslaved women created in the slave quarters for mothers was met with a sense of annoyance by White doctors, since they viewed Black midwives, medicine men, and homeopathic healers with disregard and grave suspicion.[22] Inadequate housing, lack of a proper diet, extreme work conditions, and emotional and physical abuse all contributed to poor maternal health and high infant mortality rate of Black babies. If a woman was able to carry the child to term and give birth, she still faced an uphill battle with her health because antebellum birth often resulted in serious gynecological complications.

Gynecological Complications

Antebellum birth was extremely dangerous due to the inhumane treatment of enslaved women, poor prenatal and postnatal care, and the lack of sterile, clean instruments. Consequently, women suffered from a variety of gynecological problems and birth complications such as vaginal fistulas (vaginal tears), adherent placenta, placenta retention, puerperal (commonly called childbed fever), uterine prolapse, and cesarean sections.[23] If a woman had a prolonged labor or a small pelvis that was not big enough for the child to pass through, she risked suffering a vesico-vaginal fistula, which is a tear between the wall of the vagina and bladder. Or she might suffer from a recto-vaginal fistula which is a tear between the vagina and rectum. Both conditions produced pain as well as fecal and urinary incontinence. Additionally, the use of pessaries to hold in place a prolapsed uterus caused vaginal tears. Schwartz contends that "a doctor's inexperience or ineptitude with instruments used in delivery—forceps, catheters, and the tools of craniotomy" also contributed to vaginal tears during birth.[24]

Although rare, some women suffered when the placenta did not detach from the uterine wall. Early antebellum physicians did not understand the placenta could grow into the uterine lining, muscular wall of the uterus, or through the wall of the uterus and into other organs such as the bladder or colon. However, doctors did at least understand the placenta was supposed to detach and expel in the final stage of labor. When this did not happen, women faced placenta retention. Placenta retention put women at risk of hemorrhaging, bacterial infection, or death. Doctors would try to give the body time to expel the placenta on its own, but they also prescribed ergot to stimulate contractions and enemas in the hopes of expelling the placenta. Finally, if that did not work doctors would physically remove the placenta.

First, they would insert a creosote-soaked sponge to stop any hemorrhaging and loosen the placenta. Then using their hands, they would attempt to pull the placenta loose and force it to expel. These kinds of procedures further exposed women to infections such as puerperal because the birth conditions in slave quarters were not always sterile or clean—particularly in the beginning of chattel slavery in America when aseptic methods were practically unheard of by medical professionals.

Puerperal, also called childbed fever, is a bacterial infection that originates in the uterus because of exposure to unclean birth environments. Midwives and physicians at the time did not fully understand how sterilized instruments and overall clean conditions affected the health of a mother in labor. As a result, women suffered from puerperal's side effects such as vaginal discharge, fever, and rapid pulse. According to Smith, Watkins and Hewlett, "Before 1800, women rarely survived caesarean section birth."[25] By the end of chattel slavery in 1863 when President Lincoln signed the Emancipation Proclamation, women were still suffering from bacterial infection during the postpartum period. By the late 1800s hand washing and soap was becoming part of maternal healthcare. Physicians were able to buy a bar of Ivory soap for seven cents in 1897 and there was a better understanding of the dangers of giving birth in unclean environments.[26] Unfortunately this realization came too late for many women who lived and died giving birth during America's infancy and chattel slavery. Many doctors did not realize or would not assume responsibility for being the cause of a woman's infection. In fact, White physicians could not fathom they did something to cause illness in an enslaved mother. For example, Schwartz wrote that the "Louisiana State Medical Society rejected outright the idea that physician practice could spread contagion as absurd in the extreme."[27] Enslaved women also suffered from uterine prolapse, dangerous cesarean sections, and bladder problems.

I should note that medical treatment for White people during this timeframe was also hit or miss and White women were exposed to the same dangers that enslaved Black women faced. However, the major difference in their treatment was consent, access to physicians (no matter how ill prepared) who valued her humanity and understood the privilege her position as a White woman carried in society. I suggest that maternal care during chattel slavery and after it ended is an example of White privilege in its early stages. Diangelo writes that part of White privilege is White men's occupation of the highest position possible in the race and gender hierarchy.[28] As such they have the power to decide which women matter and naturally that meant White women. And, while this may seem contradictory, because it is clear Black women had value—their value only mattered in regard to the ability to produce for slave owners. White women's wombs and the ability to bear children represented a social capital that was needed in society and they were not disposable like Black people.

I have discussed the medical culture of abuse enslaved women were subjected to, and now I would like to turn my attention to the experimentation they endured. I will briefly discuss James Marion Sims, the father of modern gynecology, because Sims represents the practices and attitudes of the time that shaped how Black mothers were treated. Understanding the poor treatment they received is important because it builds upon my theory that agency for enslaved Africans and later free Black women has been heavily controlled and influenced by the medical establishment and a national ethos that was created for Black women.

GYNECOLOGICAL EXPERIMENTATION

Perhaps no doctor of the antebellum period is more well known than James Marion Sims. Sims was a physician and slave owner who used enslaved women as test subjects to develop a surgical procedure for fixing vaginal fistulas. He also wrote extensively about placenta removal which was a common problem of antebellum childbirth. Sims's work is important to my writing because his research epitomizes the nonconsensual, dangerous, and inhumane treatment of Black women, mothers, and children. Sims received his formal education from South Carolina Medical College and Jefferson Medical College in Philadelphia. His education totaled one and a half years of training, which was on par with medical education of the day. During the early part of his career Sims conducted experiments on Black infants as he tried to find a cure for neonatal tetanus (bacterial infection) which was an epidemic among enslaved children. In one case Washington notes the brutality of his experiments when she wrote:

> He took a sick black baby from its mother, made incisions in its scalp, then welded a cobbler's tool to pry the skull bones into new positions: "During this time, I would occasionally puncture the scalp over the lambdoidal suture, with the point of a crooked awl, and prize out the edges of the parietal bones always, with the effect of greatly modifying the rigid fleur of extremities. . . ." Sims's attempt to "open" the skull was based upon a scientific myth that the bones of black infants' skulls, unlike white infants, grew together quickly, leaving the brain no space to grow and develop. This premature closing of the black skull was held to cause low intelligence and perpetual childishness in adult blacks. When the infants died, Sims castigated the sloth and ignorance of their mothers and the black midwives who attended them.[29]

Sims's extreme techniques did not produce any profound conclusions other than filthy living conditions affected illness and could be a reason for high infant mortality rates among enslaved babies. Physicians today understand enslaved children were susceptible to neonatal tetanus because of dirty living conditions and "severe calcium magnesium, and vitamin D deficiency caused by chronic malnutrition."[30] Despite this research, Sims did not blame the living conditions of the enslaved. He blamed the mothers. When Sims's research on Black infants fell short he turned his attention to female health problems and used the bodies of enslaved Black women for his scientific experiments.

Sims borrowed eleven local enslaved women from slaveholders and began conducting experimental, surgical procedures to fix vaginal fistulas. The women who were lent to Sims could not consent due to their status as chattel, nor could they request pain medication. Sims would scar the edges of the vaginal tissue and use sutures to close the wounds, but often the sutures would re-open, become infected or both, thus causing him to repeat the procedure again. Some doctors assisted Sims by holding down the women as he made incisions; however, within the first year of his surgeries many stopped attending because they could not bear the screams of the women or Sims's lack of progress in finding a solution.[31] Over the next four years Sims would invite the public and other medical professionals to watch or participate in his medical experiments. Consequently, the women were exposed to multiple surgeries.

Sims describes in his records how three women, in particular, suffered from his experiments. Anarcha, Betsey, and Lucy all endured great amounts of pain—sometimes to the point where Sims thought they would not recover. Anarcha is reported to have endured thirty surgeries. His records also show that he denied them anesthesia despite ether being available during 1840. Sims's approach to pain management was peculiar because rather than giving his enslaved patients anesthesia he addicted them to morphine by giving them large doses only after surgery. His explanation was that morphine gave patients relief from painful urination and allowed them to sleep after a long and painful surgery. Washington suggests that Sims's use of morphine was more about control than about patient comfort. Anesthesia was available, and he could have administered it during any of the surgeries.[32] His refusal to use anesthesia only extended to Black women because he provided it to White women without issue. It is unclear if other physicians refused anesthesia when using enslaved women as part of their surgical research, but it's clear that many doctors used slaves in their medical experiments.

Nathan Bozeman used four enslaved women in his button suture procedure experiment. Medical writing for the period was full of reports that mentioned enslaved persons. While some argue that we cannot hold them accountable for being men of their time and their experiments were for the greater good, there seems to be some ambivalence within the medical community regarding how they want to remember Sims and his contemporaries. I contend these doctors were willing participants in creating and maintaining a culture that dehumanized Black women for financial gain. The lack of respect for Black life is deeply entrenched in the field of medicine because for so long the enslaved were robbed of their personhood, which left them open to the abuses of medical professionals and plantation owners.

In chapter 3, "The Legislative Decisions Governing Black Wombs," I discuss the legislative decisions that controlled Black women's reproductive rights by connecting them to the controlling images of breeder, mammy, matriarch, unwed, welfare queen, teen mother, and pregnant, crack addicted mothers. I discuss how these images were used in tandem with specific laws to govern the reproductive health of enslaved women and later free Black women.

NOTES

1. Michael Guasco, "The Misguided Focus on 1619 as the Beginning of Slavery in the U.S. Damages Our Understanding of American History," *Smithsonian Magazine*, September 13, 2017, https://www.smithsonianmag.com/history/misguided-focus-1619-beginning-slavery-us-damages-our-understanding-american-history-180964873/.
2. George Lakoff and Mark Johnson, *Metaphors We Live By* (Chicago: University of Chicago Press, 1980).
3. Ibram X. Kendi, *Stamped from the Beginning: The Definitive History of Racist Ideas in America* (New York: National Books, 2016).
4. Kendi, *Stamped*.
5. Kendi, *Stamped*, 23.
6. Kendi, *Stamped*, 23.
7. Kendi, *Stamped*, 24.
8. Harriet A. Washington, *Medical Apartheid: The Dark History of Medical Experimentation on Black Americans from Colonial Times to the Present* (New York: Anchor Books, 2006), 36.
9. Dorothy Roberts, *Killing the Black Body: Race Reproduction, and the Meaning of Liberty* (New York: Random House, 1997), 23.
10. Teun A. van Dijk. "Discourse and the Denial of Racism," in *The Discourse Reader* eds. Adam Jaworski and Nikolas Coupland (New York: Routledge, 1999), 541–558.
11. van Dijk, "Discourse," 542.
12. Sara Mills, *Discourse* (New York: Routledge, 2004), 95.
13. Washington, *Medical Apartheid*, 43.
14. Washington, *Medical Apartheid*, 36.
15. Washington, *Medical Apartheid*.
16. Washington, *Medical Apartheid*, 38.
17. Marie J. Schwartz, *Birthing a Slave: Motherhood and Medicine in the Antebellum South*, (London: Harvard University Press, 2009). Harriet A. Washington, *Medical Apartheid: The Dark History of Medical Experimentation on Black Americans from Colonial Times to the Present* (New York: Anchor Books, 2006).
18. Washington, *Medical Apartheid*, 38.
19. Schwartz, *Birthing*, 19.
20. Schwartz, *Birthing*, 98.
21. Schwartz, *Birthing*, 235.
22. Schwartz, *Birthing*; and Washington, *Medical Apartheid*.
23. Schwartz, *Birthing*, 235.
24. Schwartz, *Birthing*, 235.

25. Philip W. Smith, Kristin Watkins, and Angel Hewlett, "Infection Control Through the Ages," *American Journal of Infection Control* 40 (2012): 35–42, 37.
26. Smith, Watkins, and Hewlett, "Infection Control Through the Ages," 35–42, 38.
27. Schwartz, *Birthing a Slave*, 200.
28. Robin Diangelo, *White Fragility. Why It's So Hard for White People to Talk About Racism* (Boston: Beacon Street Press, 2018).
29. Washington, *Medical Apartheid*, 62–63.
30. Schwartz, *Birthing a Slave*, 62.
31. Washington, *Medical Apartheid*, 65.
32. Washington, *Medical Apartheid*.

Chapter Three

The Legislative Decisions Governing Black Wombs

PERSONHOOD AND THE ROOTS OF PROSLAVERY DISCOURSE

Personhood is a key concept that I want to unpack as I discuss the ever-changing position Black women occupied within America's power structure. Personhood is integral to this discussion because one might argue that America's founding fathers and generations of lawmakers never intended enslaved Africans or free Blacks to be constitutional rights holders. A review of the historical evidence of our nation's founding documents and subsequent laws provides strong evidence for this intended exclusion. Some might suggest that these men perhaps foresaw and approved of an eventual end to slavery, but they did not favor it in their own lifetimes. This is quite plausible since fifty years before the end of American chattel slavery White men formed the American Colonization Society (ACS) and resettled around 12,000 freeborn Blacks and former enslaved Blacks in what would become the nation of Liberia in 1847.[1] Little cites the reason for this action was to mitigate the problem of freeborn Blacks existing in America. Some members of ACS did not think freed men and women could exist alongside enslaved men and women, and keep peace with White citizens.[2] But nonetheless the foundation for the expansion of chattel slavery was set in motion based on the laws of this land and specifically the way in which personhood is defined. At its simplest definition, personhood refers to a member of the human species. In terms of legality, personhood "denotes a person's status as a constitutional rights holder, entitled to the protective auspices of the rights contained in the U.S. Constitution."[3]

The question of personhood is a well thought out concept starting with the Declaration of Independence. Arguably the most famous line from the Declaration of Independence states, "We hold these Truths to be self-evident, that all Men are created equal, that they are endowed by their Creator with certain unalienable Rights, that among these are Life, Liberty, and the Pursuit of Happiness."[4] This line is oft repeated when people discuss what American democracy means for its citizens, but we must remember that the Declaration of Independence, like the Constitution of the United States was not inclusive of Native people, women, or enslaved persons. It was written by and for White men.

Despite the work of abolitionists, America had a distinct proslavery discourse which was present in the language of governing documents like the Constitution, the three-fifths compromise, Fugitive Slave Act, Missouri Compromise, and the Supreme Court's Dred Scott ruling. For example, the three-fifths compromise allowed states to count three out of every five slaves as one person when calculating Electoral College votes. The Fugitive Slave Act of 1793 and 1850 made it legal to capture and return runaway slaves to their owners, and the Dred Scott case sealed the fate of both enslaved and free Blacks in America. In 1846 Dred Scott filed a freedom suit against his owner and reasoned that because he traveled and lived in free states with his owner he and his family were in fact free due to a clause in the Missouri Compromise that prohibited slavery. Scott won his first case; however, Scott's owner appealed, and the case went to the Supreme Court. I decided to share Chief Justice Roger Taney's opinion at length here because it demonstrates how the Black body was viewed from a historical, legal perspective in American society. Taney wrote the following:

> The words "people of the United States" and "citizens" are synonymous terms and mean the same thing. They both describe the political body who, according to our republican institutions, form the sovereignty and who hold the power and conduct the Government through their representatives. They are what we familiarly call the "sovereign people," and every citizen is one of this people, and a constituent member of this sovereignty. The question before us is whether the class of persons described in the plea in abatement compose a portion of this people, and are constituent members of this sovereignty? We think they are not, and that they are not included, and were not intended to be included, under the word "citizens" in the Constitution, and can therefore claim none of the rights and privileges which that instrument provides for and secures to citizens of the United States. On the contrary, they were at that time considered as a subordinate and inferior class of beings who had been subjugated by the dominant race, and, whether emancipated or not, yet remained subject to their authority, and had no rights or privileges but such as those who held the power and the Government might choose to grant them.
>
> In discussing this question, we must not confound the rights of citizenship which a State may confer within its own limits and the rights of citizenship as a member of the Union. It does not by any means follow, because he has all the rights and privileges of a citizen of a State, that he must be a citizen of the

United States. . . . Consequently, no State, since the adoption of the Constitution, can, by naturalizing an alien, invest him with the rights and privileges secured to a citizen of a State under the Federal Government, although, so far as the State alone was concerned, he would undoubtedly be entitled to the rights of a citizen and clothed with all the rights and immunities which the Constitution and laws of the State attached to that character.

In the opinion of the court, the legislation and histories of the times, and the language used in the Declaration of Independence, show that neither the class of persons who had been imported as slaves nor their descendants, whether they had become free or not, were then acknowledged as a part of the people, nor intended to be included in the general words used in that memorable instrument. It is difficult at this day to realize the state of public opinion in relation to that unfortunate race which prevailed in the civilized and enlightened portions of the world at the time of the Declaration of Independence and when the Constitution of the United States was framed and adopted. But the public history of every European nation displays it in a manner too plain to be mistaken.

They had for more than a century before been regarded as beings of an inferior order, and altogether unfit to associate with the White race either in social or political relations, and so far inferior that they had no rights which the White man was bound to respect, and that the negro might justly and lawfully be reduced to slavery for his benefit. He was bought and sold and treated as an ordinary article of merchandise and traffic whenever a profit could be made by it. This opinion was at that time fixed and universal in the civilized portion of the White race. It was regarded as an axiom in morals as well as in politics which no one thought of disputing or supposed to be open to dispute, and men in every grade and position in society daily and habitually acted upon it in their private pursuits, as well as in matters of public concern, without doubting for a moment the correctness of this opinion.[5]

The most important document in American society clearly articulated the position of enslaved and free persons. They were never intended to be persons; therefore, they were not citizens who could access the rights of this nation to redress their problems. Taney described them as inferior and whether free or slave they were never to be considered citizens of this country. He also wrote no state in the union had the right to bestow citizenship on enslaved Africans, and White men did not have to respect them as persons because they were slaves for their own benefit. Taney concludes that White people's view of Blacks was fixed and universal among civilized Whites.

As we consider the tone that was set for this country, people do not discuss the psychological implications of years and years of legislative policy that controlled the interactions between Blacks and Whites. Even though the 13th Amendment abolished slavery, the 14th Amendment gave newly free Blacks citizenship and equal protection under the law, and the 15th Amendment gave Blacks the right to vote, these laws did nothing to abate the deeply rooted hate, distrust, and poor opinion of Black people that had been woven into the social fabric of American life. I share all of this because it is the unseen power of written discourse (language) that would go on to influence laws governing Black women's sexuality and reproductive rights. These laws, like the ones I mentioned earlier, come from the same space of control and repression that is evident in our country's founding documents and early laws. The subjugation of enslaved Africans is the building block for further abuses that take place after slavery ends.

These abuses are supported by the cultural discourse of America that is White supremacist, proslavery and anti-Black in nature. American discourse is deeply rooted in the concepts of freedom and revolutionary ideas where White men are gatekeepers to power in society and the founding documents of this country show that. Education reinforces ideological domination, and it is my position that medical discourse along with proslavery discourse set the tone for how Black people would be perceived regarding citizenship and personhood in America. This was accomplished by the founding fathers' control of the written discourse of the time. As privileged White men, they were able to name, organize, and *other* Black people using legislative and medical discourse heavily influenced by scientific racism. My discussion here addresses the larger issue of how Black bodies have been historically used to meet the needs of American society.

In the rest of this chapter I discuss the specific laws that affected Black women's sexuality and reproductive rights. I have chosen to organize these laws according to the time period and matched each time frame with the corresponding image from the bad Black mother trope. Enslaved reproduction and the creation of the mammy and breeder woman covers 258 years starting with the beginning of chattel slavery and ending with the Emancipation Proclamation and Reconstruction. Next, I focus on the timeframe of 1900 to 1959 where the eugenics and feminist movements played a role in setting the tone for reproductive rights of women. It is during this time frame that the image of the matriarch and welfare queen developed. Next, I explore the written laws and images of 1960 to 1989 where birth control became legal and family planning was center stage for Black families. Finally, I discuss the criminalization of Black mothers that dominated the 1990s by exploring the image of teen mothers, crack addicted mothers, and incarcerated mothers as an extension of the bad Black mom thesis.

1619–1877: Enslaved Reproduction Mammy and Breeder Woman

From 1619 to 1877 the first laws written to control the reproductive rights of slaves emphasized breeding. During these 258 years the image of the mammy and breeder woman were used in conjunction with scientific racism to justify the control of Black women's wombs. Each slave holding state had laws that restricted the ability of slaves to fully articulate family life. For example, South Carolina laws stated a child could be sold away from a mother no matter the age, and slave holders had moral authority of all their slaves. The laws of the time prevented men and women from other plantations to court each other and were used to force enslaved persons into sexual encounters with mates chosen by slaveholders. Slave marriages were not recognized by law and any children that came from the union belonged to the wife's owner. Rape was not recognized as a punishable crime and neither was statutory rape. Any child conceived from rape belonged to the woman's owner and she could not press charges.

The choices of physicians along with slaveholders cemented three opinions in American culture about Black women: (1) Black women's bodies had value if their sexuality and wombs were controlled; (2) they were not intellectually capable of caring for themselves nor their children; and (3) they were not to be considered persons with any rights either as women or as citizens of America. These points are the foundation on which Black women's ethos was built. Once America banned the import of stolen Africans, enslaved mothers bore the sole responsibility of maintaining the slave population of America. Because slave owners needed babies, a new layer of medical propaganda was added to the culture of chattel slavery—one that focused on stereotyping Black women as breeders with insatiable sexual appetites or asexual mammies.

The breeder woman was responsible for sustaining the slave economy by breeding children, working in the field and/or doing domestic work in the big house. A woman was considered fertile if she had at least one child and a *breeder* if she was able to birth multiple children over the course of her childbearing years. Enslaved women typically had their first child by age 21 and sometimes earlier depending on circumstances. Black women of childbearing age were worth considerably more than barren women, and it was common knowledge at slave markets that women who had multiple children sold for higher prices. For slave owners breeding was a smart business investment. Thomas Jefferson suggested women who were able to bear children every two years were more valuable than a man; therefore, a woman was a sound investment if she could have children.[6] Many slaveholders favored this opinion, for example, in thirteen years one Virginia slave-owner turned an $800.00 investment into a $4,000 gain because the two slaves he purchased had nine children.[7] Another slaveholder told his nephew to invest in Negro women because he managed to have 15 children in six years.

It was common knowledge among slaves that women who bore multiple children were treated better. Pregnant women received additional food, clothing, and reduced workloads as incentives for pregnancy.[8] Having multiple children was also somewhat of a protection against being sold away from family. It ensured she would be valued as an important community member. However, pregnancy did not protect enslaved mothers from hard labor or violence. A pregnant woman typically worked until her fifth or sixth month of pregnancy, and if there was a need to physically reprimand her, she would lie face down with a hole dug for her belly to receive a whipping across her back. In addition to physical violence, enslaved mothers endured medical experiments at the hands of doctors who did not value their humanity.

Mammy is the second of five controlling images that I borrow from the research of Black feminist scholars. The mammy image is an asexual Black woman who is faithful, obedient, and committed to her White family. Mammy's behavior is representative of how the ideal Black woman should act when dealing with the White power structure. Mammy's behavior was used for teaching the acquired immunity of behavioral deference to her children. Collins acknowledges this when she states:

> The mammy image is important because it aims to shape Black women's behavior as mothers. As members of the African American families who are most familiar with the skills needed for Black accommodation, Black women are encouraged to transmit to their own children the deference behavior many are forced to exhibit in mammy roles. By teaching Black children their assigned place in White power structures, Black women who internalize the mammy image potentially become effective conduits for perpetuating racial oppression.[9]

Collins's definition of mammy is useful because it sheds light on the educational role mammy played in transmitting acquired immunities to her children. This "knowledge" represents a complex dichotomy. On one hand, mammy shows deference and care to her White employer to earn income for her family, but on the other hand, she is not fully committed to encouraging her children to participate in the dance of submission. Collins highlights researchers' Barbara Christian and Bonnie Thornton Dill's argument that some Black domestics who embodied the mammy image for their White employers "discouraged their children from believing that they should be deferent to whites and encouraged their children to avoid domestic work."[10]

The mammy image is also central to upholding the oppressive financial structures of Reconstruction and Jim Crow that kept Black women employed as domestic help. After slavery, the Black body still had to serve a White economy. Therefore, Black women who were no longer slaves were now grouped as domestic help and the mammy attitude was necessary for survival in a free, albeit White supremacist society. Because mammy is thought to show more concern for her "White family" than she does her own, the misconception that Black mothers do not have the same level of care and concern for their children as their White counterparts was continued from the narrative of chattel slavery.

The medical establishment of the antebellum era had a continuum of violence that affected the value of Black women and children. It is my conclusion that the breeder woman and mammy images created an archetype for Black mothers who were necessary for the advancement of a slave class and plantation economy. After the war ended and Reconstruction took hold of the country breeder and mammy followed Black mothers into a new era. During Reconstruction 1877 to 1899 (22 years) these images served as a means for further exploiting Black families. However, during this time frame the image of the breeder woman was used to justify the beginning stages of White America's interest in limiting the Black fertility. We can be assured that Black women still had children during Reconstruction; however, it was on their own terms because they were not reproducing for a slaveholder. As free Blacks entered into the disadvantageous economic system of sharecropping having a large family was both a curse and blessing. Large families meant the workload could be shared among many and thus more production could take place. However, larger families also meant more mouths to feed and clothe and a bigger financial burden to meet. Sharecropping was not a system meant to allow newly freed Blacks the economic independence they needed. The promise of forty acres and a mule from the Freedmen's Bureau Acts of 1865 and 1866 never materialized for former slaves. During slavery Black women were forced to reproduce for the economic gains of the slave economy, but as newly freed women there was a push by the eugenics movements to control their reproduction by forcing them *not* to have children.

1900–1959: The Eugenics Movement and the Making of a Matriarch

To further the *othering* of Black mothers, the image of the Black matriarch was created to shoulder the responsibility for the breakdown of the Black family which was fostered by White society.[11] The years 1900 to 1959 represent a time in America when the Great Depression, Word War I, Word War II, and the Feminist, Birth Control, and Civil Rights Movements shaped the reproductive politics of women's lives. Between 1900 and 1910 the eugenics movement built an entire movement around the narrative of *saving* America from degenerates such as poor Whites, Blacks, and immigrants who were not fit to procreate. For example, during the presidency of Calvin Coolidge, the Immigration Act of 1924 (National Origins Act) was passed with the intent to "curtail the number of 'inferior' children born in the United States as American citizens" by reducing the number of non-Nordic persons immigrating to America.[12] The eugenics movement also demonized physical features associated with nonwhites and suggested that other races were biologically inferior. Eugenicists built upon prior proslavery discourse that made popular the belief that Black skin, wide noses, and coily hair were abnormal and were antithetical to Anglo-Saxon standards of beauty and therefore should be wiped out. Eugenicists demonized Black parents and mothers as sexually irresponsible and unfit for the task of raising productive children. Eugenicists used terms like *heredity degeneracy, hereditary defectives, undesirable, genetic profiles, bad genetics, good genetics, laziness, mental retardation, intelligence,* and *immoral habits* to describe people who should not have children. Books and journals like *Hill Folk: Report on a Rural Community of Hereditary Defectives, The Kallikak Family, The Passing of the Great Race, The Bell Curve, Heredity in Relation to Eugenics,* and *Readers' Guide to Periodical Literature* coupled with the visual rhetoric of movies like *Black Stork* gave start to a movement that would use forced sterilization as population control. As eugenics grew popular Americans across the nation joined organizations such as the Human Betterment Association, the American Eugenics Society, and American Genetics Association.[13] Prominent Americans began urging the nation to take seriously the need for population and immigration control. One such American was Margaret Sanger. Although her initial foray into eugenics was concentrated on birth control options and her early writing focused on women finding their power through reproductive choice, the message eventually turned to controlling the reproductive rights of Black women once she became associated with eugenics.

Margaret Sanger

In 1921 the nation witnessed the rise of Margaret Sanger, a women's liberation and birth control advocate who wanted women to control their own bodies. Working as a public health nurse in New York Sanger was exposed to women with multiple children and poor health conditions. Sanger's early advocacy focused on contraceptives and she argued that if women could have a contraceptive that did not depend on a man's cooperation then she would be able provide a better standard of living for herself and her children. In her 1922 eugenics missive *The Pivot of Civilization* Sanger turned her attention from contraception and women's liberation to regulating "poor, immigrants, and black Americans."[14] Sanger's complicated relationship with the eugenics movement and race is difficult to process and some of her most controversial quotes have been used out of context. For example, Sanger writes that Negroes "still breed carelessly and disastrously, with the results that the increase among Negros, even more than among whites, is from that portion of the population least intelligent and fit, and least able to reach children properly."[15] The direct quote from Du Bois's piece "Negroes and Birth Control" states the same with slight changes in wording. Du Bois writes, "On the other hand, the mass of ignorant Negroes still breed carelessly and disastrously, so that the increase among Negroes, even more than the increase among whites, is from that part of the population least intelligent and fit, and least able to rear their children properly."[16] It is not my intention to debate Sanger's intent, but her contributions need to be acknowledged because poor, Black families faced negative stereotypes from Black intellectuals of the time. Sanger's work was legitimized by president of Fisk University Charles S. Johnson, W. E. B. Du Bois, Adam Clayton Powell Jr., and Dr. Martin Luther King Jr. They understood reproduction as part of racial uplift and believed Sanger's work could benefit poor Blacks from creating families they could not afford. As such, they helped spread her message of eugenics within the Black community. With the support of these voices, Sanger advocated for the "Negro Project," which was established to serve Black women who were denied access to city health services.

I must note that the denial of services from White physicians coincided with laws restricting midwife services and access across the south.[17] These laws limited Black women's access to maternal care and pushed them into the hands of Sanger's family planning centers that were seen with skepticism from Black communities. These experimental "family planning centers" were thought to be a test ground for covertly promoting eugenic principles in the Black community. Because birth control was eventually conflated with the desire to control the reproductive rights of a certain group of women, historians struggle with Sanger's contributions to the feminist movement. Some reproductive scholars argue that Sanger was a birth control advocate at her core and her racist ideologies were reflective of the times in which she lived more so than it was a desire to wipe out the Black population. So, while her support of the eugenics movement gave all women access to birth control, it also opened the door for forced sterilization of poor women of Eastern European and African American descent.

During the twentieth century, politicians used the language of the eugenics movement to frame population control as a pressing issue and across the country laws were passed that controlled the reproductive rights of Americans deemed unfit. In 1907, Indiana passed an "involuntary sterilization law, empowering state institutions to sterilize, without consent, criminals and 'imbeciles' whose condition was 'pronounced unimprovable' by a panel of physicians."[18] "By 1913 twenty-four states and the District of Columbia passed laws forbidding marriage by people considered genetically defective, including epileptics, imbeciles, paupers, drunkards, criminals and the feebleminded."[19] By 1914 seven other states passed involuntary sterilization laws and by 1927 thirty states had compulsory sterilization laws for people who were considered mentally unfit, feeble minded, had genetic defects or were on welfare.

In addition to their mantra that only the best of society should procreate, eugenicists lobbied against social programs that would help poor people. This prompted politicians to create laws that would limit people's access to public assistance and encourage and or force them to get sterilized. One such politician was David H. Glass of Mississippi. In 1958 Glass introduced legislation to force sterilization on welfare recipients. Glass argued that this would discourage sex outside of marriage. Glass's law passed the Mississippi House of Representatives but failed to pass in the Senate. Even though Glass's law failed the fact that it was even written and passed in the House is an indication of the support that politicians and regular citizens had for compulsory sterilization. All across the county state and local governments had sterilization programs. For example, in North Carolina, my home state, 73 out of 100 counties had sterilization programs that did not end until 1974. Washington reports 70,000 to 100,000 people were sterilized by government funded programs in the mid to late twentieth century and many of those persons were Black men and women.[20] This was achieved by opening birth control clinics in Black communities and subjecting Black men and women to compulsory sterilization. Thousands of Black men were castrated in this country and while my research focuses on Black women I would be remiss if I did not mention how castration was used as a solution for population control and as a form of punishment for criminal acts.

Eugenicists picked the continued denigration of a Black mother's sexual relationships as a way to control her access to Aid to Families of Dependent Children (AFDC) support. Originally AFDC was part of the 1935 Social Security Act and was developed to meet the needs of poor people over the age of 65, the blind, and fatherless children. By 1960 most AFDC recipients were single mothers with kids and increasingly more Black Americans began to use the service as unemployment skyrocketed. When Black Americans started to utilize the AFDC, politicians purposely suggested the program was only serving the needs of Black families. So, to penalize women with illegitimate children states passed the controversial "man in the house rule." The law prohibited a woman from receiving aid if she was living with or involved with a man that was not the father of her children. The man she was dating or thought to be having a sexual relationship with, or a stepfather was now responsible for providing financial support for her children. Women's sexual relationships were put on display and her choices were judged by politicians and social workers. For example, one such law suggested that the regulation apply only to sexual intercourse that happened once a week, another suggested sex every three months and then it was suggested that once every six months was a reasonable amount of time. Law makers struggled with the absurdity of these caveats and rewrote the laws to ensure they could maintain control of Black families' lives. Women were often forced to hide relationships so they could maintain their assistance. However, in 1968 the Supreme Court ruled the law was contrary to the purpose of the AFDC program. AFDC was originally part of the Social Security Act of 1935.

This idea that Black women continued to have babies without regard to their ability to care for them is a stereotype that follows her to this day, but we must consider the societal forces that worked against Black mothers and families and the stereotypes of mammy, breeder woman, and matriarch. When Black women were property, their children represented cheap, free labor and were needed. After slavery ended Black women and children were recast as burdens on American society. The same women who were once responsible for supporting the economy of America with their wombs were now responsible for destroying the economic stability of America with her children. The image of the mammy and matriarch proved useful in creating a discourse that showed working, Black mothers as neglectful, angry, and ill prepared for the job of mothering.

Mammy's transformation from house slave to domestic worker and the development of the matriarch became popular images for Black women and mothers in the mid to late part of the twentieth century.[21] According to Collins, the matriarch is a failed mammy who does not show deference and appropriate gender behavior in a White patriarchy.[22] The Black matriarch is the starting point for the contemporary image of the bad Black mother trope. She is as an absent mother who works constantly; therefore, her children are left unattended. She is a problem because her femininity is not shrouded in submissiveness and deference to the White power structure. Although her employment outside the home contributes to the support of the Black family, her ability to generate income, when her man cannot (due to racist employment practices) is held against her. While she is praised when her children do well, she is blamed for their failures. And when her children do fail, she bears the burden of blame alone.[23] Society criticizes her relentlessly for any mistakes and focuses its attention on what she has done wrong and not on the generational issues of poverty, access, and class.[24]

In addition to raising children that are a problem for society, the matriarch is responsible for the breakdown of the Black family. Her aggressive, harsh, unfeminine, and emasculating nature is cited as the cause for Black men's absence in the home. Therefore, she is the reason why patriarchy cannot take root in the family and why Black men cannot assume their role within American patriarchal society. But this argument is exhausting and impossible! How can Black women be responsible for the breakdown of the Black family, when generational poverty and oppression are written into the laws of the land? Unjust laws, a criminal system that values bodies more than rehabilitation, little to no healthcare, substandard housing that leads to health problems, high unemployment rates, poor funding for schools that serve Black families, and White privilege which silently maintains White supremacy in this country all work against the Black family structure.

Together mammy, breeder, and matriarch support the next image of domination tied to the reproductive rights of Black women—the unwed, welfare queen. My own view is that this image, in particular, further problematized the bad Black mother trope more than the images of mammy, breeder, and matriarch. The unwed, welfare queen is an example of what happens when Black women's wombs are not restrained and the financial burden of raising children is placed on the government.

1960–1989: Using the Unwed, Welfare Queen to Control Black Wombs

During the 1960s and 1970s there was a shift in the narrative about Black mothers and their relationship with the state. As the 1960s ended the focus on limiting Black reproductive life was more prominent than ever and laws were passed connecting a woman's ability to receive aid with her willingness to take birth control or be sterilized. Politicians started calling Black women *unwed mothers* and later *welfare queens*. Unwed mothers of any race were problematic for the White, male patriarchy; however, Black women posed a bigger problem. White, unwed mothers had the option to place their children into the adoption system. If she was willing to give up her child, the repercussions of her sexual misconduct would be wiped from the record and she could go on to be a productive citizen in White America. This choice allowed middle-class, White families to absorb the child into the fabric of White America, thus adding value to society. Black women did not have this option. For starters, foster care and adoption services were not available to Black families until 1930, and unwed, Black mothers were characterized as bad mothers who should be punished for creating babies that were "expensive and undesirable."[25] The idea that she could become a productive member of society if she gave her child up for adoption was preposterous because bad Black mothers didn't add value to society by having unwanted children. And, policymakers did not assist or encourage Black families in the adoption system once it was available to the Black community.[26]

Additionally, there was a misconception among politicians and social workers who believed Black families did not wish to adopt other people's children, which is not true. The Black community, since chattel slavery, embraced the West African principle of community childcare to survive the tearing apart of families. As such *other mothers* and fictive kin became part of the Black familial experience very early in our community's existence in America.[27] The narrative of the unwed mother was the precursor to the welfare queen. I combined the two into one image because it is important to distinguish between two parent families that lived in poverty and needed public assistance and unwed, Black mothers who needed public assistance.

The unwed, welfare queen is portrayed as being satisfied with collecting welfare from the state, which makes her an affront to the economic stability of America. Her detractors claimed she lacked the morals to raise productive children and her uncontrolled sexuality resulted in multiple children the state would pay to raise. Her choices prevented her children from benefiting from an intact family unit comprised of a working father and mother. The government used the unwed, welfare queen image as justification for controlling Black women's reproductive rights. This image was used to force Black women who received government assistance into compulsory sterilization programs that were initially started by eugenics or using birth control like the intrauterine device (IUD), Depo-Provera, or Norplant.

Compulsory Sterilization

Eugenicists argued that the government had the right to enforce sterilization if a parent was receiving public assistance. Illinois, Iowa, Ohio, and Virginia all drafted legislation that would connect recipients' benefits to their reproductive rights. Louisiana and Mississippi managed to pass laws that made having more than two illegitimate children a crime. Mandatory sterilization proposals connected to welfare were all over the country and eventually fell out of favor with the public; however, Black women were still the victims of government paid doctors who believed that sterilization was an appropriate contraceptive for poor, Black women and girls. Sterilization continued well into the 1960s and eventually ended in most states around the late 1970s.

Roberts shared that in the 1970s sterilization became the most common form of birth control in the United States and across the South. It seems that J. Marion Sims was not just the father of modern gynecology. He was also the father of nonconsensual, medical experiments on Black women. He left a culture of disregard for Black women and medical experimentation because some two hundred years later, again, we have White doctors using Black women's bodies, without consent, for their own personal research agendas and gain. And both northern and southern states sterilized Black women. In the North, it was often done under the auspices of "teaching opportunities" for medical residents.

The assumptions about Black women and their fecundity was one reason why so many Black women were sterilized by government paid physicians and many of those doctors who conducted sterilizations had troubling opinions about Black women having children and the public assistance they received. For example, researcher Gena Corea writes, "Dr. C, chief of surgery at a northeastern hospital, for example, gave Corea his opinion that "a girl with lots of kids, on welfare, and not intelligent enough to use birth control, is better off being sterilized." 'Not intelligent enough to use birth control,'" Corea added, "is often a code phrase for 'black' or 'poor.'"[28] Another doctor explained the justification for violating patients' autonomy, "As physicians we have obligations to our individual patients, but we also have obligations to the society of which we are a part . . . the welfare mess . . . cries out for solutions, one of which is fertility control."[29] These quotes reveal the long prevailing negative attitude against Black mothers and their right to control their wombs or consent to medical procedures. Some doctors did not bother to covertly conduct these surgeries they would bully and pressure women into being sterilized. For example, Dr. Pierce was the only obstetrician in Aiken Country, South Carolina that accepted Medicaid patients. Pierce's disdain for Black mothers with multiple children was tied to his belief that he was paying for these women's children via the public assistance they received. He threatened 20-year-old Marietta Williams that he would not deliver her third child unless she agreed to being sterilized. When Williams did not acquiesce to his demands, he is quoted as saying "Listen here, young lady, this is my tax money paying for this baby and I'm tired of paying for illegitimate children. If you don't want this sterilization, find another doctor."[30] Roberts reports that women across the South were subject to abusive threats from physicians if they came from large families or they themselves had too many children.[31]

As Black families became weary of medical procedures and the White medical establishment, they turned to organizations like the Southern Poverty Law Center (SPLC) to help redress their concerns regarding forced sterilization. The SPLC filed a class action law suit and discovered an estimated 150,000 poor women were sterilized in federally funded programs across the South and nearly half of them were Black.[32] Most, if not all, of these sterilizations were paid for with government funds under Medicaid which happened to be the "only publicly funded birth control method readily available to poor women of color."[33] Eventually forced sterilization was replaced with other contraceptives like the birth control pill, intrauterine device (IUD), Depo-Provera, and Norplant. The pill was made legal in 1965 for married couples, but unwed women were initially denied access to the pill. However, three years later the birth control pill was made legal for all women—regardless of marital status. In 1968 the IUD was introduced as a contraceptive; however, it proved to be dangerous for women. Infections and deaths were reported, and the IUD was taken off the market, but not before it had been given to thousands of women who used inner city clinics for their health needs. Depo-Provera was introduced in 1963 and was originally created to treat cancer, but somewhere along the way it was used on healthy women as a contraceptive. The FDA withdrew support when it was discovered it caused cancer in healthy Beagles (the dog). By the time is was pulled 4,700 women of Native and African American decent had already used the drug as a contraceptive. These experimental contraceptives ruled the 1960s, 1970s, and 1980s and Black women on public assistance were targeted, used, and sometimes forced as test subjects. Politicians, social workers, and medical professionals felt these measures were necessary to slow the birth of Black children.

The image of the unwed, welfare queen was so powerful in the American psyche that the medical field seemed ok with the risky contraceptives Black women were being given. During the late 1980s life for Black Americans had improved somewhat, but many still lived in impoverished cities all over rural and urban America. The late 1970s and 1980s gave rise to hip hop culture which exposed the problems and aggression of the inner-city life to White, middle class America and the politicians that represented them. This cultural shift is important to note, because hip hop musicians boldly described the racism, drugs, crime, and violence that permeated their lives. It also gave politicians fuel for reinventing how Black mothers would be viewed, thus a new group replaced mammy, breeder, matriarch, and the unwed, welfare queen. Moving forward the teen mom, crack addict mother, and incarcerated mother were used to continue the subjugation and control of Black women's sexuality and reproductive rights in the latter part of the twentieth century and early part of the twenty-first century.

1990 and Beyond: Teen Mothers and Pregnant Crack Addicted Mothers

As America started to acknowledge the poverty of inner cities and rural counties, politicians' focus was placed on the systems of class, race and access in an attempt to devise new policies that would further criminalize Black mothers living in poverty. Again, written discourse played a role in how America was to see this next generation of mothers. Politicians used coded language to describe Black communities and phrases like *inner-city, inner city youth, fatherless, welfare mother, welfare queen, welfare babies, crack babies, crack mothers, teen mom, culture of poverty*, and *urban poor* became synonymous with Black women and children.[34] It was during the late 1980s and 1990s that the image of the teen mom and crack addict mother emerged as controlling images of Black motherhood.

Brenda's Got a Baby: Teen Moms

Much has been written about the hyper-sexualized image of Black women, so I will not repeat that here. Rather I want to focus on the hyper-sexualized image of the Black teen mother. It is not my intention to discuss why young women ages 15 to 19 end up pregnant and the social circumstances that affect their lives regarding sexual encounters. Although important, there has been enough research about this topic and it is evident, to this day, that our communities both Black and White struggle with teen pregnancy. In many ways the stigma attached to teen pregnancy, at least for White girls, has been removed thanks to shows like *16 and Pregnant, Teen Mom, Teen Mom OG, Gilmore Girls, Reba,* and *The Secret Life of Teenagers*. Each show features a White cast that normalizes the experience of teen pregnancy from a White, middleclass and or working-class perspective. I should note that these shows have several seasons and Black women and other women of color have been included, but the representation is minimal at best. This speaks to how the media continues to lift White mothers. What is usually a stigma (teen pregnancy) aims to show that White teenage mothers are deserving of redemption and a second chance whereas Black teen mothers are still seen as a drain on the system.

Suffice to say—Black adolescent mothers struggle because of a myriad of reasons, and like their mothers before them, "they are deprived of every resource needed for any human being to function well in our society: education, jobs, food, medical care, a secure place to live, love and respect, the ability to securely connect with others."[35] My interest in adolescent mothers lies with understanding how language and visual imagery shifted to include teen mothers as part of the bad Black mother thesis. My discussion of Black teen moms addresses the larger matter of how and why she is used for the benefit of racists' political agendas, and finally I am interested in the laws written based on the assumption that teen mothers are a financial drain on America's resources.

The term *teen pregnancy* became a common term in the 1960s but it was not until the mid-80s that teen pregnancy became a topic of interest with politicians and social scientists.[36] In addition to these terms Oscar Lewis's phrase *culture of poverty* became associated with Black families receiving public aid. These words were added to the existing discourse about Black mothers and opened the door for poverty to be a sort of subculture within American society. Lewis' *culture of poverty* theory suggests that rather than figure out how to change or escape poverty, people adapt and learn how to survive, which becomes a part of their cultural experience. Lewis and others like Daniel Moynihan described poverty as a pathology Black women pass to their children, thus creating generational poverty and a breakdown in family structure. The increase of teen mothers coupled with the decrease in Black marriage, to Moynihan, was an indication that Black mothers were not doing their jobs properly.[37] The problem with this line of thinking is that it overlooks the institutional and systemic problems that exacerbate poverty in a capitalist society and it does not acknowledge the 400 year (1619–1960) toll White supremacy had on Black families.

The image of pregnant, Black teens was used as another justification for forcing contraceptives on women as well as restricting public aid benefits. Since Black babies were a threat to America, Black women's sexuality had to be controlled at all costs and this included Black girls' sexuality and reproduction. According to politicians and many in society the Black teen mother was just like her mother. She was promiscuous, lazy, irresponsible and unwilling to raise children who would become productive members of society.[38] She would emasculate her man, give into her unbridled sexual needs and refuse to restrain her reproduction if she was not stopped. From Moynihan's perspective, "Black teen age girls' morals are different from those of mainstream society because they do not have strong moral values prohibiting sexual activity at an early age and before marriage."[39] Moynihan and others feared that if not stopped Black teens would continue the cycle of babies and dependence on public aid. Moynihan's theory suggests Black women were to blame because as Collins contended in her book *Black Sexual Politics*, it is one thing to be a poor, working class woman who cannot make ends meet, but it is another thing when that same woman is fertile and has the potential to pass her poverty and moral behaviors to her children—specifically daughters.[40]

Teen Mothers, Racist Political Agendas, and ADFC

The regulations surrounding welfare changed with the whims of politicians. During the Reagan era welfare became racialized whereby Black mothers and teen mothers became the face of America's teen pregnancy crisis. President Reagan used the Black family and teen moms to justify cutting ADFC funding. In 1996, economists reported that teen pregnancy cost taxpayers $8.9 billion a year.[41] By racializing welfare and turning Black reproduction into a threat against America's economic prosperity Reagan's War on Welfare connected the image of ADFC to Black wombs. And, politicians argued teen mothers were repeating the cycle of sexual irresponsibility and poverty by having children they could not financially support. Reagan's sweeping cuts limited who could receive welfare payments, limited income calculations, and reduced the age of eligibility for children from 21 to 18.[42] To further reduce benefits, states also factored in housing subsidies, food stamps, and income tax credits before awarding benefits.[43] Thanks to Moynihan's report and the existing narrative about Black mothers and now Black teen mothers four prevailing assumptions became circulated truths in American society: (1) teen mothers viewed ADFC as the only financial source they were interested in having; (2) teen mothers were lifelong recipients of welfare; (3) teen mothers were morally corrupt and did not believe having a child at a young age as problematic; and (4) the Black community was fine with teen mothers having babies.[44] However, to Elaine Bell Kaplan these assumptions simply were not true.

Kaplan described with detail the struggle adolescent mothers faced from the government, their families, and society in her book *Not Our Kind of Girl*. Kaplan's survey participants described a system that was demoralizing to their self-esteem and prohibitive of encouraging or even allowing economic growth. According to Kaplan, in 1990 fifty percent of teen mothers age nineteen and younger received their income from welfare. On average a mother with one child could potentially receive a monthly total of $498.00 in ADFC benefits to cover rent, food, clothing, diapers, formula, transportation, laundry, and miscellaneous expenses. The notion that welfare equates to *living one's best life* or that welfare is a lifelong aspiration for young mothers is a ridiculous assertion by politicians. Living off welfare benefits is economically and socially challenging.

Many of the women in Kaplan's study discussed how additional income reduced their benefits. If mothers worked or did not participate in government ordered job training programs they risked having their benefits decreased. A reduction in benefits made it virtually impossible to work, find reliable childcare, safe housing, or attend school, yet many of these mothers used welfare as a temporary support. The constant regulatory changes in welfare also precluded some mothers from receiving their same level of benefits as they worked to change their financial conditions by working, participating in job training programs, or receiving child support. The one good point mothers mentioned from ADFC were the health benefits their children received.

Receiving child support was another challenge to a mother's ADFC benefits. Under the Child Support Enforcement Act of 1975 women were required to establish paternity before claiming child support. Housing was another problem that affected their benefits. Many mothers lived with relatives to make ends meet, and landlords did not want to rent to teen mothers let alone mothers who received welfare. One participant in Kaplan's study waited nine years to receive an apartment in government housing. Despite these challenges researchers found that for most families "chronic or near-chronic welfare dependency was the exception rather than the rule."[45] Most mothers used ADFC benefits immediately after their child's birth or when they were faced with medical conditions and job loss.[46] Truthfully "the rules and regulations of ADFC operate to sustain the prejudices of the 'respectable elements of society.'"[47] This notion of welfare dependent families is another asinine suggestion when we consider all the roadblocks that impede a successful transition from welfare to self-sustainability. In addition to potential cuts in their benefits and being stereotyped as welfare scam artists, teen mothers had to deal with dehumanizing office administrators who were gatekeepers to benefits.

The process of securing welfare and interacting with office administrators was stressful and demoralizing. Women in Kaplan's study reported having to share intimate details about their sex life to receive assistance. Application questions included when, where, how often, and with whom they had sex. All this was done to shame them for their choices and make the process of received aid degrading. Women reported being talked down to by social workers and finding it hard to navigate the required paperwork. The lack of education and resources these women had also contributed to others' perception of them. The ongoing narrative about their desire to cheat the system and have unprotected sex in exchange for a monthly check affected their self-esteem. Mothers in Kaplan's study reported using tactics such as dressing up, recreating their personal narrative, and avoiding being spotted in welfare related establishments to mitigate the shame and embarrassment they felt. If the stress of dealing with resentful and overworked ADFC employees was not enough often these mothers faced public shame from their families and external community.

Critics of the Black community suggested Black families were happy to welcome child after child born without any resources in place. What I find ironic is that the same negative attitude White America had about Black mothers and welfare, the Black community exhibited toward Black, teen mothers. Participants in Kaplan's study of teen mothers living in Oakland, California revealed their communities condemned and ostracized them as "scheming, lazy, 'welfare cheats,' who used their bodies as baby-making machines for profit."[48] Participants stated they were stared at, gossiped about, and shunned when people would discover they were mothers. When the conversation turned to religion, participants shared they were told they would not be forgiven for the sin of having a child out of wedlock. Kaplan suggests the Black religious community was concerned with status and class which could be one reason for the ongoing debate about responsibility for the downfall of the Black community.[49] The ongoing debate is circular and shifts blame from *the man*, the system of racism, to Black men, to Black mothers and finally to teen mothers. For me the question of who is to blame for the trouble in the Black community is situated in the notion of respectability politics where wealthy and middle-class Blacks police the behaviors of community members to assimilate and gain respect of the dominate culture—read White.

What I have described thus far is an image of an adolescent mother who was used by politicians to show that Black womanhood was antithetical to White patriarchy's view of motherhood. She became a scapegoat for welfare reform and the Black middle class's reason for the continued breakdown of the Black community. And while others were crying foul about the choices of these young women, another epidemic was sweeping poor communities across the nation—crack. The introduction of crack in the 1980s and the devastation it caused by the end of the 1990s further criminalized Black mothers and added another image to the bad Black mother trope.

The Crack Epidemic & Incarcerating Crack-Addicted Mothers

Crack cocaine hit the streets of America in the late 1980s, and by the mid-1990s cities all over the country were struggling with an addiction crisis. Crack was popular because the high was intense and the product was cheap. Crack's low cost made it the drug of choice for addicts who could not afford to purchase more expensive drugs like heroin or powder cocaine. As crack spread across the country, it ravaged communities that were already poverty stricken and health professionals witnessed a dramatic increase in the number of women giving birth to children who were addicted to the drug. In 1989, the height of the epidemic, it was estimated that close to 375,000 children were born each year with the drug in their system.[50] The rhetoric of medical professionals rang alarm bells all over the country and report after report told stories of children who were doomed to a life of hardship and health problems.

Medical experts suggested children exposed to crack would suffer long term neurological disorders as well as birth defects and cerebral and cardiac abnormalities.[51] The immediate effects of a child's exposure to crack included withdrawal seizures and low birth weight. Even though the research was grossly overstated, and the public had some sympathy for these children, people were more outraged by the actions of addicted mothers than the misrepresentation of the medical data. For many Americans the image of the welfare queen and now crack addicted mothers further criminalized Black mothers. No longer were they just welfare queens who defrauded the government, they were now drug addicts giving birth to the next generation of Black children who would further drain the American economy. My analysis presumes that women of color were disproportionally represented in drug court because of their already high level of contact with government services and politicians' desire to penalize Black women for being both addicted to crack and pregnant. By using negative images of Black mothers and adding pregnant addicts to the bad Black mother thesis, Reagan's War on Drugs and War on Welfare prompted politicians to pass laws prosecuting prenatal and perinatal drug use. Changes in the law were rooted in the argument that fetal rights took precedence over maternal rights.

The War on Drugs meets the War on Welfare: Prosecuting Prenatal and Perinatal Drug Use

In 1982 President Reagan declared a war on drugs. He continued in the footsteps of previous presidents who sought to control the flow of illegal drugs into American cities. To receive public support politicians and legal professionals created a panic around the crack epidemic and overused the term *crack babies*. Arguing that pregnant crack users needed to be stopped to protect the unborn, child prosecutors began pushing for legislation that would incarcerate non-violent drug users and pregnant mothers. Passing laws that put users away was not difficult because the American public was already propagandized to see drug use as part of urban crime culture, which was outside the reach of White suburbia; however, to enforce what they called *protective incarceration*, prosecutors had to get creative to arrest pregnant drug abusers. Prosecutors charged women with child abuse, delivery of drugs to a minor via the umbilical cord, possession of a controlled substance, assault with a deadly weapon, contributing to delinquency of a minor, and homicide if the child tested positive for drugs and later died.[52] This was achieved thru collaborative efforts between police agencies, medical facilities, and social service offices.

One example of such collaborative effort took place in South Carolina. Charleston, South Carolina law enforcement and the Medical University of South Carolina's (MUSC) Interagency Policy allowed medical staff to conduct nonconsensual drug testing on pregnant patients receiving maternal health care at MUSC. Staff reported any positive drug tests to police and police used the information to arrest mothers on child abuse charges. If a woman tested positive, she could choose to enter a treatment program or decline treatment and go to jail. Medical staff only had to *suspect* a woman was using drugs and staff could order a drug screening—without her knowledge. This selective screening or profiling, as I like to call it, is biased. At their personal discretion medical staff had the power to control who was selected for testing. This is particularly disconcerting given that some medical staff already had a poor opinion of Black and or addicted mothers. Consequently, a good portion of MUSC's clients were poor, Black women, which made them disproportionally represented in the program. In total 42 women were arrested and only one was not Black.[53] Across the nation the fact that most screening tests happened in hospitals where low-income patients frequented automatically increased the number of African American women selected for testing. The Center for Reproductive Justice argued prosecutors focused too much on crack users which unfairly targeted inner-city users—often Black women.[54]

In defense of their actions prosecutors argued that arresting drug-addicted mothers ultimately protects the fetus; however, some courts began to see punitive measures as counterproductive. A total of 22 states overturned prosecutions of women for their actions while pregnant because defense attorneys and judges started questioning the legality and ethics of drug testing mothers without their consent and the civil rights of the mother versus the civil rights of the fetus. The culture of surveillance in the Black community, which dates to chattel slavery, still affirms America's obsession with controlling and watching Black bodies and communities, which is why medical facilities were able to test pregnant users without their permission and ultimately incarcerate so many Black mothers.

The competing interests of fetal rights versus a mother's civil rights fueled the argument that *protective incarceration* was best for the child. Placing fetal rights over the rights of mothers is a slippery slope. Incarceration limits a woman's access to medical care, nutrition, and family support. If a mother complains of pain prison officials are slow to react which could be dangerous for the mother and child. For example, on July 31, 2018, Diana Sanchez was recorded on closed circuit TV at a Denver, Colorado jail, seeking assistance as she went into labor.[55] When prison officials ignored her pleas for help she ended up delivering her son alone, without medical assistance. The material reality of being incarcerated means being exposed to harsh conditions that can negatively affect a woman's pregnancy and as an argument, the prenatal conditions are not a valid point for improper care in jail. One of those conditions is being shackled or handcuffed. The use of shackles and handcuffs, according to Roberts, was a common practice, for crack addicted mothers. For example, Lori Griffin was handcuffed and placed in leg irons during her weekly prenatal visits with her doctor and she was handcuffed to the bed during labor.[56] The abuse pregnant women endure at the hands of the court system and prison industry is reminiscent of the abuse enslaved mothers endured at the hands of White slave owners. Rather than looking at drug use as an illness, and these women as sick, these women were described as exchanging their maternal instinct for crack. Further, the media's portrayal of pregnant crack addicts as "irresponsible and selfish" meshed well with the existing image of Black mothers who were already devalued by society. A Black, pregnant crack addict is antithetical to the good mother thesis American society has constructed. She is not married, middle class, White, or using her body as a healthy vessel for the nurture of her child. And, since she is Black her ability to rise to the level of White motherhood diminishes because of her race, poverty, and drug use. Black crack addicts add to the ongoing rationale for society to control the reproductive rights of Black mothers.

Because of the crack epidemic, women were arrested, jailed and separated from their children at an alarming rate. The increase of women in the prison system during the 1980s and 1990s is a direct correlation to how crack use was viewed as a criminal activity and not an illness requiring treatment. As a result, both the users and the sellers were incarcerated with the intention that jail time would serve as a *treatment facility* for addicts. It would be naive to deny that race did not play a role in how the crack epidemic was constructed for public consumption, but it did. The evidence is found in how government officials and news outlets describe today's drug culture and current opioid crisis.

The National Institutes of Health (NIH) describes opioid addiction as a dependence on prescription pain medicine, heroin, and synthetic opioids like fentanyl.[57] While politicians are reluctant to admit that race affects the resources allocated to deal with our current opioid crisis, I believe the current crisis has been contextualized around saving White, suburban mothers who started out with a prescription for pain medication. As such, drug addiction is now described as an *illness* that needs treatment. For pregnant users, there are treatment options that allow them to work through their addiction instead of separating them from their children. There are even programs that allow mothers to keep their young children with them for a period of time while they are incarcerated. For example, shows like *Pregnant in Prison*, *Pregnant Behind Bars*, and *Born Behind Bars* highlight the struggles mothers have with addiction. There is an ongoing debate about why the opioid crisis is depicted as only affecting White America when addicts of color are affected too, and I'm not interested in that debate, drug use is drug use. Rather, I am interested in the response of policy makers who see this as a public health emergency and are responding with funding for treatment programs.

With the support of President Donald Trump, a commission on combating drug addiction and the opioid crisis was convened. The tone is totally different from how the crack epidemic was described. President Trump declaring this a national public health emergency under federal law meant that federal funding could be used. In the Commission's 2017 report, Chair Governor Christie's language indicates a need for "treatment services to be improved, foremost by developing thoughtful national evidence-based standards of care, record-keeping, and long-term support."[58] Christie uses language that is inclusive and not exclusive when he uses the following phrases:

- "Our people are dying."
- "I know you will win this fight for the people who elected you."
- "It is time we all say what we know is true: addiction is a disease."[59]

Working in conjunction with the Commission is the NIH and they too have contextualized the opioid addiction with much softer language. Through its program Helping to End Addiction Long-Term (HEAL), the NIH identified 26 research priorities aimed at stopping the opioid crisis in America. Greater emphasis was placed on supporting a trial program called neonatal opioid withdrawal syndrome (NOWS) and following a cohort of pregnant women from all of over the country for 10 years in order to study the effects of NOWS.[60] I mention this because in order to follow these women and their children, one assumption is that they are not being punished for their drug use. Rather they are being given an opportunity to work through their addiction and the addiction their children are born with. Overall the language used for this epidemic describes a softer, less aggressive drug crisis. This is a marked difference from how President Ronald Reagan responded to the flood of crack and increase of crack users. The irony is that the crack epidemic was precipitated by Reagan's support of drug dealing Contras who used drugs to fund their regime.[61] Reagan's response was a War on Drugs that took aim at poor communities by placing the blame on families for their addictions. However, when Black mothers were in the throes of the crack epidemic the country responded with criminal charges and incarceration.

CONCLUSION

The field of obstetrics owes a deep debt to the countless enslaved women who suffered through a variety of medical experiments. Because of their sacrifices White doctors were able to test medical hypotheses, track the progress of disease and cures, and develop surgical practices that benefited all women. In the written laws and community discourse of American society, we can see how major moments in American history were tied to defining images for Black Women. The laws were written to ensure Black families would be precluded from a functioning family structure. These laws also demonstrate how discourse can be used to create and control a reality based on racism, social constraints, and community membership. They show how unethically written texts can contribute to the dehumanization of humanity.

For Black mothers the material reality of a negative, socially constructed reality has long-lasting effects. It is evident in how the language used presented Black motherhood as the polar opposite of the standard of American motherhood—read White. The breeder woman and mammy represent chattel slavery and antebellum south. Once out of slavery Black women were recognized as mothers only because their wombs were no longer controlled by slave owners; therefore, the language describing her also changed. She was now a mother—but a matriarch responsible for poverty in the Black community and the absence of Black men in the home. The Black matriarch and unwed, welfare queen was used during the early part of the twentieth century to justify the control of Black women's reproductive rights, and the Black teen mother and crack addict mothers were used as an extension of the bad Black mother thesis that permeated the 1980s and 1990s. Her changing image in the mass media also contributed to a cycle of negativity that affected her financial, social, medical, and political well-being. The misrepresentation of Black women's lives often undergoes makeovers with the changes in American society and it has been my goal in this chapter to show how the images of breeder, mammy, matriarch, welfare queen, teen mother, and pregnant user work within American discourses to control the reproductive rights of Black women.

In chapter 4, I discuss the institution of American motherhood as a contested space influenced by the ideologies of patriarchy, technology, and capitalism.[62] In doing so, I also explore how the ethos of motherhood was used to racialize and exclude Black women from the narrative of American motherhood.

NOTES

1. Becky Little, "How a Movement to Send Freed Slaves to Africa Created Liberia," April 5, 2010. *History.com*, https://www.history.com/news/slavery-american-colonization-society-liberia. Accessed 4.16.2020.
2. Little, "How a Movement."
3. Zoe Robinson, "Constitutional Personhood," *The George Washington Law Review* 84:3, vol 84 (2016):606–667, 613.
4. Thomas Jefferson et al., July 4, Copy of Declaration of Independence. July 4, 1776. Manuscript/Mixed Material. https://www.loc.gov/item/mtjbib000159/.
5. Chief Justice Roger Taney, "Opinion of the Court." *Dred Scott v. Sandford*, 60 U.S. 393 (1856), 405–407, https://www.law.cornell.edu/supremecourt/text/60/393. Accessed December 12, 2019.
6. Dorothy Roberts, *Killing the Black Body: Race Reproduction, and the Meaning of Liberty* (New York: Random House, 1997), 24–25. And Marie J. Schwartz, *Birthing a Slave: Motherhood and Medicine in the Antebellum South* (London: Harvard University Press, 2009), 68.
7. Marie J. Schwartz, *Birthing a Slave: Motherhood and Medicine in the Antebellum South* (London: Harvard University Press, 2009), 68.
8. Patricia Hill Collins, *Black Feminist Thought: Knowledge Consciousness, and the Politics of Empowerment* (New York: Routledge, 1991).
9. Collins, *Black Feminist Thought*, 72.
10. Collins, *Black Feminist Thought*, 73.
11. Collins, *Black Feminist Thought*, 73.
12. Loretta A. Ross and Rickie Solinger, *Reproductive Justice: An Introduction* (Oakland: University of California Press, 2017), 31.
13. Roberts, *Killing*.
14. Roberts, *Killing*, 59.
15. Roberts, *Killing*, 77.
16. W. E. B. Du Bois, "Black Folk and Birth Control," *Birth Control Review* 16.6 (1932).
17. Loretta Ross, "Reproductive Justice as Intersectional Feminist Activism." *Souls* 19, no. 3 (2017): 286–314, 289.
18. Dorothy Roberts, 1997. *Killing the Black Body: Race Reproduction, and the Meaning of Liberty* (New York: Random House, 1997), 67.
19. Roberts, *Killing*, 65.
20. Harriet A. Washington, *Medical Apartheid: The Dark History of Medical Experimentation on Black Americans from Colonial Times to the Present* (New York: Anchor Books, 2006).
21. Collins, *Black Feminist Thought*, 68.
22. Collins, *Black Feminist Thought*, 68, 75.
23. Collins, *Black Feminist Thought*.
24. Collins, *Black Feminist Thought*.
25. Rickie Solinger, "Race and "Value": Black and White Illegitimate Babies, 1945–1965," in *Mothering, Ideology, Experience, and Agency*, ed. Evelyn Nakano Glenn, Grace Chang, and Linda Rennie Forcey (New York: Routledge, 1994), 298.
26. Solinger, "Race and "Value," 298.
27. Collins, *Black Feminist Thought*, 119.
28. Roberts, *Killing*, 92.
29. Roberts, *Killing*, 92.
30. Roberts, *Killing*, 92.
31. Roberts, *Killing*, 92.
32. Roberts, *Killing*.
33. Roberts, *Killing*, 97–98.
34. Washington, *Medical Apartheid*, 209.
35. Elaine Bell Kaplan, *Not Our Kind of Girl: Unraveling the Myths of Black Teenage Motherhood* (Berkeley: University of California Press, 1997), 10.
36. Loretta I. Winters and Paul C. Winters, "Black Teenage Pregnancy: A Dynamic Social Problem," *SAGE Open* 1–14 (2012).

37. Elaine Bell Kaplan, *Not Our Kind of Girl: Unraveling the Myths of Black Teenage Motherhood* (Berkeley: University of California Press, 1997), 131.
38. Collins, *Black Feminist Thought*, 76.
39. Elaine Bell Kaplan, *Not Our Kind of Girl: Unraveling the Myths of Black Teenage Motherhood* (Berkeley: University of California Press) 1997, 4.
40. Patricia Hill Collins, *Black Sexual Politics* (New York: Routledge, 2004), 130–131.
41. Elaine Bell Kaplan, *Not Our Kind of Girl: Unraveling the Myths of Black Teenage Motherhood* (Berkeley: University of California Press, 1997), 5.
42. Adriane Bezusok, "Criminalizing Black Motherhood." *Souls* 15:1–2 (2013): 39–55.
43. Bezusok, "Criminalizing,"46.
44. Elaine Bell Kaplan, *Not Our Kind of Girl: Unraveling the Myths of Black Teenage Motherhood* (Berkeley: University of California Press, 1997), 143.
45. Kaplan, *Not Our Kind*, 143.
46. Kaplan, *Not Our Kind*, 143.
47. Kaplan, *Not Our Kind*, 131.
48. Kaplan, *Not Our Kind*, 133.
49. Kaplan, *Not Our Kind*, 4, 159.
50. Dorothy Roberts, "Punishing Drug Addicts Who Have Babies: Women of Color, Equality, and the Right of Privacy," *Harvard Law Review* 104, no. 7 (May 1991):1410–1482.
51. Enid Logan, "The Wrong Race. Commiting Crime, Doing Drugs, and Maladjusted for Motherhood: The Nation's Fury Over 'Crack Babies,'" *Social Justice* 26, no. 1(1999): 115–138, 117.
52. Center for Reproductive Rights. 2016. "Research Overview of Maternal Mortality and Morbidity in the United States," *Black Mamas Matter* (New York: Center for Reproductive Rights, 2016), 2.
53. Dorothy Roberts "Unshackling Black Motherhood," *Michigan Law Review*, 95 no. 4 (February 1997): 938–964.
54. Center for Reproductive Rights. 2016. "Research Overview of Maternal Mortality and Morbidity in the United States," *Black Mamas Matter* (New York: Center for Reproductive Rights, 2016), 2.
55. Kevin Bliss, "Lawsuit: Woman Gave Birth Alone in Colorado Jail Cell," Prison Legal News, October 7, 2019. https://www.prisonlegalnews.org/news/2019/oct/7/lawsuit-woman-gave-birth-alone-colorado-jail-cell/.
56. Dorothy Roberts, *Killing the Black Body: Race Reproduction, and the Meaning of Liberty* (New York: Random House, 1997), 943.
57. National Institutes of Health, "NIH HEAL Initiative Research Plan," March 18, 2020, https://www.nih.gov/research-training/medical-research-initiatives/heal-initiative/heal-initiative-research-plan.
58. Chris Christie, "The President's Commission on Combating Drug Addiction and the Opioid Crisis," *The Presidents Commission*, November 1, 2017, 90, https://www.Whitehouse.gov/sites/Whitehouse.gov/files/images/Final_Report_Draft_11-1-2017.pdf.
59. Christie, "The President's Commission," 5.
60. National Institutes of Health, "NIH HEAL Initiative Research Plan."
61. Michelle Alexander, *The New Jim Crow: Mass Incarceration in the Age of Colorblindness* (New York: The New Press, 2012).
62. Barbara Rothman, *Recreating Motherhood* (New Brunswick: Rutgers Univeristy Press, 2000).

Chapter Four

Ideology, Ethos, and Silence

Much has been written about the experiences of Black mothers, but what has not been fully discussed is how ideology and ethos affect Black maternal health and the reproductive rights of Black women. American history and media outlets have conditioned the public to see Black mothers and the loss of Black life as *so what* moments. When people see yet another Black mother on television crying about her dead children,[1] some segments of America do not see a grieving mother. Rather, they see a Black woman who was unfit to be a mother crying over a child that she corrupted. Consequently, the media creates a narrative that criminalizes victims and dehumanizes Black mothers. It is my belief that in addition to hospital negligence when treating early warning signs (infection, raised heart rate, or internal bleeding), Black mothers die, in part, because of the implicit biases attached to a specific image of Whiteness, Blackness, and motherhood.

In this chapter, I discuss why the ideology of motherhood and related ethos are important to the Black maternal health conversation taking place today. I do this by first defining American ideology and then the ideology of motherhood to understand how identity, which I suggest is an extension of ethos, supports oppressive power structures in society. Next, I draw on the works of rhetorical scholars to discuss the ethos of White and Black motherhood. I talk about why these ethos were created and how they became embedded, circulated truth(s) in America's cultural memory. As I continue to unpack ethos, I then move into a discussion of the rhetoric of silence and listening as I find them both productive ways of thinking about Black women's voice, agency, and survival.

AMERICAN IDEOLOGY

Ideologies are systems of beliefs that give people parameters for how they interact with the world. Ideologies are supported by written, oral, and visual discourse and have the power to shape the attitudes, goals, interests, and motivations of societies. Herndl argues that knowledge is socially constructed and legitimized through language and rhetorical activity.[2] Fairclough emphasizes that ideologies are closely linked to power and language and further suggests that ideology is a way to maintain unequal power relationships.[3] American ideology, from its inception, was a combination of religious, patriarchal and racist practices that were anti-woman, anti-Native, and anti-Black. Mixed in with these ideologies was a fierce promotion of the concepts of freedom and democracy supported by the Declaration of Independence, the United States Constitution, the Bill of Rights, and centuries of racist and sexist laws (discussed in chapter 2). These documents along with chattel slavery set the tone for the social stratification of people across race, gender, and class. Collectively, segments of American discourse dehumanized and restricted the lives of enslaved Africans and later free Blacks. As such, the concept that Black lives were disposable unless in service to White America affected every facet of Black life—including maternal ideology.[4]

Ideology and the Institution of Motherhood

Motherhood scholars advance maternal theory from three perspectives: motherhood as experience/role, which is centered on conception, pregnancy, childbirth, and breastfeeding; motherhood as an institution/ideology, which explores the cultural underpinnings that affect how motherhood is seen in society and how it is used to ensure patriarchal control; and motherhood as identity/subjectivity, which focuses on the criteria that control who is considered a legitimate mother.[5] My discussion of motherhood addresses all of these perspectives because to discuss Black motherhood means addressing the experience, the ideology, and the ethos/identity she embodies in America. To understand ethos, I first begin with the ideologies (patriarchy, technology, and capitalism) that influence and complicate how we understand the institution of motherhood.

The Influence of Patriarchy on Motherhood

American patriarchy teaches that the nuclear family (father, mother and children living together) is the only legitimate family structure. The promise of a nuclear family was used to control White women's sexuality and was meant to ensure she would not ruin her opportunity to marry and have children within the boundaries of a "proper" marriage. I should note that in traditional African society, a nuclear family was not the standard structure. Families were communal, and men and women depended a great deal on extended family members for support. Because Black families were disrupted by slavery, enslaved communities in some ways adapted the communal nature of African villages. The difference was the circumstance that forced them into this kind of living condition. In addition to a communal family structure, African women exercised a great deal of control in their communities and matrilineal power was not uncommon. For example, in some royal families heirs to the throne passed through the female lineage and not the male. For Black, enslaved women, family structure was different. She was unable to enter into a nuclear family because her body was meant for work—much like a machine or a tool.

The Influence of Technology on Motherhood

Feminist scholars writing about pregnancy posit that the ideology of technology encourages society to view pregnant bodies as objects to control and monitor. Rothman and Seigel remark that the use of monitoring technologies such as transvaginal and abdominal ultrasounds, fetal monitors, blood tests, and C-section delivery treat mothers like machines that must deliver a baby in the most efficient, predictable and rational way possible.[6] Birth then becomes something that should happen the same way, each time, for every woman—like how a machine operates—rather than an organic process with a level of unpredictability. Pincus suggests, "[T]he mainstream US culture's attitudes toward birth devalue women's bodily experiences, classifying them according to a mechanistic model of care."[7] Furthermore, Seigel adds that the use of technology alongside medical, cultural, and philosophical considerations downplay women's humanity.[8] In addition to these concerns, the scientific advances of today's world have changed how we understand conception. Pinto-Correia's work traces the development of assisted reproductive technologies (ART) such as surrogacy, in vitro fertilization, and egg donation which has changed how a child is conceived and our understanding of child custody.[9] The notion that the human body, if managed properly, can operate like a finely tuned machine also extends to today's expectations of labor and delivery—and one of the reasons why so many women, both Black and White, experience complications. Comprehending birth from a technological approach has serious consequences for women because the time needed to give birth becomes controlled by doctors' schedules, hospital costs, and insurance payouts. The ideology of technology and pregnancy have a direct correlation to capitalism and the understanding that bodies and time are commodities to be managed.

The Influence of Capitalism on Motherhood

Within a patriarchal society American capitalism as an ideology treats the body as a commodity. As such, women are valued and commodified based on their ability to provide men with sexual intercourse and/or children. Women of any ethnicity can satisfy the sexual urges of men; however, according to Rothman, only "healthy White babies" were valuable; therefore, White women have more value.[10] In her assessment, Rothman overlooks the commodification of Black mothers and children. Black mothers and healthy Black children were considered valuable for the financial growth of America. While patriarchy, technology, and capitalism affect the treatment of mothers, I add there is a powerful ethos influencing the ideology associated with motherhood.

ETHOS

Ethos, when translated from Greek, means character. Thus, to be a good speaker one needs to embody the forms of virtue, which Aristotle describes as "justice, courage, temperance, magnificence, magnanimity, liberality, gentleness, prudence, wisdom."[11] An Aristotelian approach to ethos includes: phronesis, which is the demonstration of knowledge about a topic; arete, which is the moral explanation of one's argument; and eunoia which is the goodwill and rapport one has with the audience. Early scholars of rhetoric have varying opinions about ethos, and Baumlin suggests there are two scholarly traditions concerning ethos. The Isocratic tradition focuses on the true character of the speaker and argues that the speaker must be honorable in nature before he can attempt to persuade.[12] Aristotelian tradition focuses on how a speaker constructs his character and suggests that giving the appearance of being good in order to persuade is enough. The presumption that speakers are in control of their ethos does not make room for the nuanced way ethos is created—especially for marginalized groups who find themselves part of narratives they did not create. From a classical point of view, most will readily agree that character and the forms of virtue are indeed important and that ethos does not exist in isolation but is embedded in the social expectation of a community. Where this agreement usually ends is when women and African-American scholars of rhetoric posit that classical rhetorical theory overlooks the lack of agency and voice denied women, Black women, and Black communities.

Ethos and Women Rhetors

When discussing the rhetorical tools of women, Donawerth asserts that early women rhetors used religious text to redefine women's authority and right to speak; rhetorical skills from the classical canon to support their claims; letter writing, conversation, and preaching to convey their message; reimagined gender roles; and deconstructed women's roles as listeners.[13] Nedra Reynolds suggests that ethos starts with the self-identity of the "individual agent as well as the location or position from which that person speaks or writes."[14] Ethos is deliberate, meaning the speaker has the power of choice and represents more than good morals; "it is a complex set of characteristics constructed by a group, sanctioned by that group, and more readily recognizable to others who belong to and share similar values or experiences."[15] For Johanna Schmertz, like other scholars who draw on feminist epistemologies, ethos is more than a tool for persuasion. It operates on a continuum where women reimagine how they enter into a rhetorical space—situating the location based on the subjectivity they created which reflects their world, politics, and existence.[16]

Black Women Rhetors and Ethos

Similarly, to the experiences of women, African American rhetors and scholars of rhetoric understand that ethos is limited because the rhetorical choices available for Black expression were often controlled by the White imagination.[17] Shirley Wilson Logan's research on African American women's rhetoric found an emphasis on abolition, women's rights, anti-lynching, racial uplift, literacy, and social reform. Women like Mary Shadd, Sarah Redmon, Frances Watkins Harper, Mary Cary, Maria Steward, Sojourner Truth, Ida B. Wells, Lucy Smith, Josephine Ruffin, Victoria Matthews, Fannie Williams and Anna Julia Cooper were the early nineteenth-century voices for Black women. As these women became rhetors in their own right, they understood the need to create an identity that was of their own making. Fannie Williams and Anna Julia Cooper both focused on the progress of Black women after slavery and encouraged other Black women to redefine their womanhood outside of the existing model provided by White society. Williams used identification and arrangement to show that Black women were not different than White women.[18] She also demanded that Black women be respected irrespective of class, and she also stressed a common womanhood among all women. Anna Julia Cooper was less conciliatory than Fannie Williams in her approach to remaking Black women's ethos, and she was not interested in a comparison between the merits of Black women and White women in regard to embodying the virtues of womanhood. Cooper took aim at new Black academic patriarchs like Douglass, Washington, Du Bois, Crumwell, and Grimke. She felt it was important to address the false assumptions of superiority and wanted these men to get on with the business of highlighting the needs of Black women. Cooper's use of arrangement based her arguments in common Christian historical relevance for women.[19] The works of these early African American women demonstrate a keen understanding of the need to reimagine the self and castoff fake personas.

African American Rhetoric and Ethos

African American ethos is situated within the racialized discourse of American society that created what Morrison describes as a "fabricated African presence."[20] I find that this same fabricated presence precluded Black women from self-definition. Richard Schur writes that African Americans have been relegated to a fixed position in their ethos because of American racism and its treatment of Black people. Schur further posits that ethos is comprised of our social roles, habits, and way of life.[21] Composition scholar David Holmes probes the concept of ethos by asking who authenticates the Black voice which, to me, is a central question because for a very long time Black ethos and the right to speak was controlled by the American nation-state.

Hunter further complicates ethos by suggesting ideology can function as the ethos of a nation-state.[22] As such, America's national ethos is closely aligned with the principles of freedom, democracy, and capitalism—all of which are underscored by the need to sustain a particular social order—with White men at the top. The blurred line between ethos and ideology also requires governments and those in power to create ethos for groups of people in society. Central to the ethos and ideology of motherhood is the understanding that humans use symbols and attach meaning to these symbols as part of communication—which is rhetorical in nature. For our communication systems to have meaning, people agree with (consciously and unconsciously) a shared vision that is circulated in society. The symbols and their meaning give people the ability to "alter perception, to reinforce and channel belief, to initiate and maintain action, as well as to foster or undermine a competing ideology."[23] Often these ethoses conflict with how people see themselves. And even though marginalized people work to create an alternative, more authentic rendering of self, certain communities of people still find it hard to rebuff ethoses that are negative and controlled by the nation-state. Through the use of these ethoses governments are able to control institutional structural systems (businesses, schools, and jails), which are where power struggles are enacted.

In her article "Constructing Essences: Ethos and the Postmodern Subject of Feminism," Johanna Schmertz discusses Crowley's argument that ethos is both "situated" and "invented." Situated ethos is linked to a person's character, social position, or authority, similar to the Isocratic approach to ethos, and invented ethos is derived from the authority of a speaker's linguistic devices.[24] I agree with Schmertz's assessment of Crowley's argument regarding the invented nature of ethos; however, for Black mothers, their silence precludes them from inventing or situating their ethos within the topos of motherhood. They walk into motherhood carrying carefully constructed images of their womanhood and their abilities as a mother shaped by an ethos that has by and large been controlled by White men. Therefore, I offer that Black maternal ethos is highly subjective and based on the White patriarchy's need to control Black women's reproductive rights and stigmatize Black communities. And because knowledge is socially constructed and legitimated through language use and rhetorical activity, we cannot dismiss ethos and its role in Black women's lives.

For Black women then and now, self-definition has been an ongoing challenge. They actively engaged in the process of self-definition, by using personal experience as a rhetorical tool to build ethos. Pittman's essay "Black Women Writers and the Trouble with Ethos" suggests, like other Black scholars of rhetoric, that chattel slavery and post slavery stereotypes prevented Black women from being assigned a good ethos.[25] I agree that Black women's ethos has been hijacked by things not of their making, but a point that needs emphasizing is that ethos is really not the problem. The real problem is the assumption that all people are judged by the classical understanding of ethos without consideration for the subject positions and characterizations or caricatures that nation-states create via written discourse and media.

By creating ethos for communities of people, those in power use politically motivated rhetoric for their own purpose. For example, American politicians created an ethos about enslaved Africans that aligned with the need to keep them enslaved. As a result, enslaved persons were characterized as lazy, unintelligent, sexually promiscuous, and a myriad of other things. This became the ethos of the Black community in this country and the foundation for how White people would understand an enslaved person's role in America's caste system. Similarly, within the ideology of motherhood, those in power created two competing ethoses—a dichotomy that defined White mothers as good and Black mothers as bad.

The Ethos of Black and White Motherhood

The valorization of White motherhood is reproduced for every generation and taught through television, movies, magazines, websites, Internet searches, and pregnancy literature. A good mother is White, chaste, selfless, caring, and committed to her children and under the protection of White patriarchy. She is thin, beautiful, well dressed, and middle class. And if she is not middle class or wealthy, the White patriarchy still provides her entry into the good mother category because she is White. This characterization of motherhood with its class and beauty standards, I am sure, is oppressive for White women too, but it is so powerfully woven into the fabric of American life; we do not see how it *others* Black mothers and their experiences. The ethos of Black mothers developed from the racialized ethos which controlled the symbolic meaning attached to the image of Black mothers. Consequently, her ethos was juxtaposed against that of White women who were considered the gold standard for motherhood, and Black mothers came to represent the epitome of a bad mother. To illustrate this difference, I borrow from Lindal Buchanan's description of god-terms in her table *The Woman/Mother Continuum*.[26] Buchanan theorizes motherhood through the lens of *devil terms* and *god terms* that have either a negative or positive value attached to them. In her table Buchanan argues that words like "childlessness, work, sex, self-centered, materialism, immorality, hysteria, irrationality, extreme emotion, weakness, the sensual body, and public sphere" all have a negative association with the term *woman*.[27] She writes that *mother* has a positive association with the words "children, home, love, empathy, religion, nourishment, altruism, morality, self-sacrifice, strength, the reproductive body, protection, the private sphere, and the nation." And while I agree with Buchanan's assessment of devil terms and god terms, I do not believe these words are typically associated with Black motherhood in the larger topos of motherhood. If we take the terms Buchanan applies to motherhood, we can see how Black mothers are not able to use these positive god terms in the same way. In table 4.1, I build on Buchanan's work by applying the positive associations, but through the lens of race. I link specific images and values from the bad Black mother trope to positive associations of motherhood.[28]

In Buchanan's distinction between the negative devil term *woman* and the positive god term *mother*, we can see how the term woman can be synonymous with Black mothers.[29] I posit that these terms control who is allowed to be a legitimate mother, because the institution of motherhood is viewed through the experiences and expectations of White, heterosexual, middle class women. To this end, Black mothers and anyone outside of this narrative are erased from the landscape of motherhood. If we understand motherhood as the goal for a woman (hypothetically speaking), and White women are the standard bearers, then where does that leave Black mothers? The written discourse and imagery of the canon[30] of Black motherhood became part of America's national narrative. Based on shared stereotypical assumptions, cultural commonplaces, and a universal narrative of White motherhood, one can see how the ethos of Black motherhood was created to be an aberration—an antithesis, if you will, to the concept of a *good* mother.[31]

As I think about new ways to comprehend ethos and motherhood, I believe it is useful to theorize ethos from the role of the speaker as well as the listener. The speaker engages her audience by using Aristotle's three elements of ethos: phronesis, arete, and eunoia and is in a position of power to decide whose voice matters. This side of ethos is easily recognized because

Ideology, Ethos, and Silence 57

Table 4.1. Bad Black Mother Trope

Black Mothers in Society	Corresponding Image
Children (multiple)	Breeder woman
Single parent and fatherless homes which disrupt patriarchy	Matriarch
Her love is seen as sexual and immoral due to her unrestrained sexual appetites.	Jezebel
She has empathy (for White families via mammy).	Mammy
She does not protect her children because of her poor choices.	Crack addicted mother
She is religious but not pious because she has sex and children outside of wedlock.	Matriarch Teen mom
She cannot nourish because she is unable to provide financially for her family and she is immoral, so she is not able to provide a moral foundation for her children.	Welfare mother
Altruism: She is not self-sacrificing.	
She lacks moral training from her mother which ends up making her a teenage mother.	Teen mother
She does not sacrifice for her children.	All images
She is seen as strong and overly masculine when necessary.	Slave field hands
Her reproductive body is only valid if it supports the American economy; thus, reproducing for slave owners or curtailing her reproduction post slavery.	Breeder, jezebel, teen mother
The private sphere does not exist for her because Black bodies are policed, watched, and controlled. She will work and have her sexuality and body on display for the world.	All images
She is not of value to the nation unless her womb is controlled.	All images

the focus is on the persuasiveness of the speaker and her character. The part of ethos that is more interesting to me is the subject position and ethos of the listener. According to Critical Discourse Analysis scholar Norman Fairclough, the subject position is a role that people play in a communicative event that has specific discourse, power moves, and assumptions that dictate how participants will act. Participation requires them to draw on their members' resources which teach them how to interpret the social scene in which they are participating.[32] Who is the person listening? Does she have any power in the rhetorical exchange? Is her ethos her own, or was it created for her? Has she been silenced? Is her silence a choice or by force? How is silence manifested in the lives of Black women, and what does that look and feel like to them? These questions swirl around in my mind as what the rhetoric of silence and listening means to Black mothers' ethos.

Chapter 4
RHETORICAL SILENCE AND LISTENING

Black maternal ethos is highly subjective and complicated by the concepts of silence, listening and control. Who controls the overall rhetorical experience if silence is expected from a certain demographic of people, and if the audience cannot decline to listen or disagree, has the speaker truly persuaded them of anything? In its elementary form, silence is the absence of speech, but like love, silence comes in many forms. Silence can deliver meaning, can isolate, can be imposed on a person or group, can be self-imposed, and can be a mode of knowing.[33] Cheryl Glenn defines silence as a rhetorical practice that is unappreciated because of its association with the feminine expression. It has also been used as a trope "for oppression, passivity, emptiness, stupidity, or obedience."[34] As a rhetorical art, silence also begs the question of control and choice. According to Glenn, Bruneau identifies three types of silence. Psycholinguistic silence is a part of the natural flow of conversation that has pauses and moments of organic silence. Interactive silence is a tool where group members utilize silence to critically think and problem solve. Sociocultural silence is based on community membership and what is appropriate for a given location.[35] For example, most people understand that silence is expected in religious ceremonies or public settings like libraries and hospitals.

Glenn speaks of being muted as a practice of silencing. To be muted means one is silenced, and it implies a lack of or loss of control. Muteness typically happens to women, children, and marginalized groups. It is the "dominate group in a social hierarchy" that has the power to mute subordinate groups.[36] Once muted, the subordinate group are excluded from the formation, validation, and circulation of meaning even if the discourse is about them.

A History of Rhetorical Silence

If we consider the speech of Black women, silence is further complicated by her intersecting identities and community positions. To be clear, I am not talking about the art of conversation and the turn taking that happens when people talk naturally. I am speaking about the right to participate fully in given speech acts and the systematic silencing that happens through gatekeeping practices of the nation-state. Black women are silenced because of gender, race, and class. Additionally, if she is not heterosexual, she is also silenced because of her sexual orientation. Her silence renders her invisible and places her in a subject position where she can only listen and never respond. I find Glenn's concept of muted groups particularly useful in describing the experiences of enslaved persons. To be muted is to have one's ability to speak removed. Slaves were rendered inarticulate by the structure of chattel slavery, and those in power muted their identities as well as their voices. The subject position of chattel required complete obedience, and that meant silence unless given the permission to speak, and even when that permission was granted, they still were not able to fully participate as equals. I also envision silence as a form of self-imposed protection that Black women carried with them into the future. She, like Black men, understood when to speak and what could not be said to White people. Accordingly, her self-imposed silence became a tool for survival—a way to protect her economic livelihood and protect herself from physical violence during Jim Crow and beyond.

In her speech "The Transformation of Silence into Language and Action," Audre Lorde acknowledges the ways in which American society has always demanded silence of Black women. Lorde, so eloquently, writes that the struggle to transform silence into action is a courageous act—especially for Black women who have been rendered invisible.[37] Black women who dare to speak out are punished by being branded as loud, angry, and aggressive. This tactic is used to dismiss her message and her presence by reducing her speech to emotional gibberish and reminding audiences that she is not qualified to speak. One such instance is how President Donald Trump engages with Black women reporters. For example, he told Press Corps reporter Abby Phillip, "I watch you a lot; you ask a lot of stupid questions." When asked about reporter April Ryan, he stated, "You talk about somebody that's a loser. She doesn't know what the hell she is doing."[38] Trump's latest attack on a woman of color was Yamiche Alcindor who asked a series of questions about COVID-19. His response to her question was, "Be nice. Don't be threatening."[39] Trump's response was classic textbook silencing for Black women based on the angry Black woman trope often used by White people who do not want to see them as equals.

In addition to being silenced by the outside world, Black women find themselves silenced within their own communities if they do not align their speech with the "protect Black men or don't air our dirty laundry" mantra. She is expected to overlook the indiscretions of Black men at all costs—even at the expense of herself, and Black women who do gather the courage to speak out against Black men may find themselves vilified and turned away from the community that is supposed to represent *home*. For example, Anita Hill was written off as just another *sista* who wanted to bring a Black man down when she went public with sexual harassment claims against Clarence Thomas, and Robyn Givens was branded a liar when she went public about the abuse she endured at the hands of Mike Tyson. The women who spoke out against R&B star R. Kelly were also held in contempt for their accusations of sexual assault and rape.

I would also like to mention the unique way White women's tears silence Black people. In her book *White Fragility*, Robin Diangelo suggests that

White women's tears in cross-cultural racial encounters can be used to redirect attention away from the actual encounter in question where she is not confronted but comforted, thus, diminishing her racist and or inappropriate behavior toward the person of color.[40] For example, I was having lunch in a very popular restaurant. The store manager and assistant store manager (both White women) were involved in an employee review with a Black man. The assistant manager told the man that she did not believe him to be a team player and that he was not approachable. The man who looked to be about 40 years old responded, "I do everything you ask me to do, so I don't understand why you think I'm not a team player? I come to work on time and do my job." Instead of the assistant manager providing the man with examples of what she thought was a team player, she started crying, consequently, dismissing his response and rendering him silent. Then, the store manager finished the review while the assistant manager was dismissed to gather herself. So, the man was left wondering what he said to make her cry—which is something I also wondered. How was he going to make her feel better, which I'm sure took precedent over her concerns about his performance and how he could be a better team player?

There were many things wrong with this encounter. For starters it lacked privacy, and denial of privacy is a power move in and of itself. As a paying customer, they should not have been sitting so close to me that I could see and hear all that was said. I felt like I was in the meeting too. Second, I do not believe either of them were interested in having a *conversation* with him and were surprised that he did not agree with their assessment of his performance. As such, they were expecting his silence, and when they did not get it, she resorted to tears, which lends itself to invisibility. I should also add that I ate at this restaurant almost once a week for a year up until this incident and was familiar with the employee. He was very popular and friendly with the customers and could be seen reading his Bible on his break. Whether he was difficult to deal with I do not know, but I cannot fathom that his demeanor changed drastically when dealing with the managers—the very people who controlled his employment. In any event, I digress but with purpose. White tears are very real, and today's social media is replete with videos of White women intimidating people of color only to turn around and cry and place blame for her outburst on the person she intimidated. This encounter is also an example of rhetorical listening.

Rhetorical Listening

The rhetorical acts of silencing and listening go hand in hand. Listening has traditionally been associated with spoken language, but I would like to discuss what it means to listen and what it means to have the right to be heard and taken seriously. Rhetorical theorists have not always considered listening to be an important concept to study because of the assumption that people automatically listen in a conversation, but scholars like Ratcliff, Dreher, and Thompson argue that rhetorical listening is a valuable contribution to rhetorical studies, and I believe it to be a key area of understanding when discussing Black maternal health outcomes. When defining rhetorical listening, Ratcliff defines listening as "a trope for interpretive invention and more particularly as a code of cross-cultural conduct."[41] Furthermore, Ratcliff suggests that rhetorical listening can be used to better understand a person's intersecting identities such as race, gender, and class. Tanja Dreher's approach to listening asks us to unpack the gendered hierarchies that control who is placed in a position to listen, which can be based on the "values and esteem according different identities and cultural productions"[42] in society. Additionally, she suggests that listening as a field of study "shifts some of the focus and responsibility for change from marginalized voices and onto the conventions, institutions, and privileges which shape who and what can be heard in the media."[43]

Silence and listening still have a far-reaching effect on the lives of Black mothers. No longer is she living under the constant threat of physical violence from White men who believe she is property, although we know Black women are still vulnerable (Sandra Bland, Atatiana Jefferson, L'Daijohnique Lee, Jazmine Headley, Breonna Taylor) and our children and men are still vulnerable (Emmett Till, Trayvon Martin, Jordan Davis, Tamir Rice, Eric Garner, Michael Brown, Akai Gurley, Ahmaud Arbery, George Floyd). The act of silencing, muting, and non-listening is not as obvious as it once was. And no longer is she living under the watchful eye of overseers of the past. But we know that the hyper surveillance that renders us invisible and hyper visible exists to remind Black women that their silence is required if they are to exist in certain spaces typically reserved for Whiteness.[44] Audre Lorde speaks of how one can break a silence, but still remain silent and how to speak is to resist. bell hooks writes that she knew intuitively that talking was fine as long as she talked a "talk that was in itself a silence."[45] That is women and Black women in particular are taught to speak so that they do not offend or transgress those in power.

For Black mothers, breaking through the silence and non-listening is a matter of life and death, and it is not their responsibility to make physicians, nurses, and other health care professionals listen. It is the responsibility of the medical establishment to stop silencing Black mothers and listen to what they are saying. Ultimately, what is at stake here are lives—hers and her child's. My point about ethos, listening, and silence reinforces the belief that the power to speak and or be silenced matters in all areas of life—the private and the public, and foregrounds the next part of my discussion, which centers on how narratives are reproduced. In chapter 5, I will discuss commercially produced pregnancy books so that I may understand how ethos affects pregnancy culture and reproduces biases in the medical establishment. I discuss the data I collected from a critical discourse analysis of pregnancy literature. In my analysis I use an interdisciplinary approach that includes Ben and Martha Lee Barton's denaturalization of the natural and Critical Discourse Analysis theories of Norman Fairclough to critique ideology, ethos, and images of motherhood affecting Black motherhood.

NOTES

1. Trayvon Martin, Sabrina Fulton, Tamir Rice, Samira Rice, Eric Garner, Gwen Carr, Sandra Bland, Geneva Reed-Veal, Philando Castile, Valerie Castile, Ahmaud Arbery, Wanda Cooper, Breonna Taylor, and Tamika Palmer.
2. Carl Herndl, "Teaching Discourse and Reproducing Culture," in *Central Work in Technical Communication* ed. Johndan Johnson-Eilola and Stuart A. Selber (New York: Oxford University Press, 2004), 222.
3. Norman Fairclough, *Language and Power* (New York: Routledge, 2013).
4. Patricia Hill Collins, *Black Feminist Thought: Knowledge Consciousness, and the Politics of Empowerment* (New York: Routledge, 1991).
5. Andrea O'Reilly, *Maternal Theory: Essential Readings* (Ontario: Demeter Press, 2007).
6. Barbara Rothman, *Recreating Motherhood* (New Brunswick: Rutgers Univeristy Press, 2000), 31.
7. Jane Pincus, "Foreword," *The Rhetoric of Pregnancy* (Chicago: The University of Chicago Press, 2014), x.
8. Marika Seigel, *The Rhetoric of Pregnancy* (Chicago: The University of Chicago Press, 2014) 7.
9. Clara Pinto-Correia, "Technological Motherhood," in *Fear, Wonder, and Science in the New Age of Reproductive Biotechnology* ed. Scott Gilbert and Clara Pinto-Correia (New York: Columbia University Press, 2017), 107–126.
10. Marika Seigel, *The Rhetoric of Pregnancy* (Chicago: The University of Chicago Press, 2014), 31.
11. Johanna Schmertz, "Constructing Essences: Ethos and the Postmodern Subject of Feminism," *Rhetoric Review* 18, no. 1 (Autumn 1999): 82–91, 48.
12. James S. Baumlin and Tita French Baumlin, *Ethos: New Essays in Rhetorical and Critical Theory* (Dallas: Southern Methodist University Press 1994), xiv.
13. Jane Donawerth, *Rhetorical Theory by Women Before 1900* (Maryland: Rowman & Littlefield Publishers, 2002).
14. Nedra Reynolds, "Ethos as Location: New Sites for Understanding Discursive Authority," *Rhetoric Review* 11, no. 2 (Spring 1993): 325–338.
15. Reynolds, "Ethos," 327.
16. Schmertz, "Constructing Essences," 82–89.
17. Toni Morrison, *Playing in the Dark: Whiteness and the Literary Imagination* (New York: First Vintage Books, 1992), 6.
18. Shirley Wilson Logan, *With Pen and Voice. A Critical Anthology of Nineteenth-Century African-American Women* (Carbondale: Southern Illinois University Press, 1995), 100–106.
19. Shirley Wilson Logan, *With Pen and Voice*, 47–52.
20. Toni Morrison, *Playing in the Dark: Whiteness and the Literary Imagination* (New York: First Vintage Books, 1992), 6.
21. Richard Schur, "Haunt or Home? Ethos and African American Literature," *Humanities* 7, no. 80 (2018): 4–13.
22. Lynette Hunter, "Ideology as the Ethos of the Nation State" *Rhetorica: A Journal of the History of Rhetoric* 14, no. 2 (Spring 1996): 197–229, 198.

23. Keith Kenney, "Building Visual Communication Theory by Borrowing from Rhetoric," in *Visual Rhetoric in a Digital World* ed. Carolyn Handa (New York: Bedford St. Martin's, 2004), 332–343.

24. Johanna Schmertz, "Constructing Essences: Ethos and the Postmodern Subject of Feminism," *Rhetoric Review* 18, no. 1 (Autumn 1999): 82–91, 84.

25. Coretta Pittman, "Black Women Writers and the Trouble with Ethos: Harriet Jacobs, Billie Holiday, and Sister Souljah," *Rhetoric Society Quarterly* 37, no. 1 (Winter 2007): 43–70.

26. Kimberly Harper, "In the Fight of Their Lives: Mothers of the Movement and the Pursuit of Reproductive Justice." *Reflections: A Journal of Community-Engaged Writing and Rhetoric*, forthcoming.

27. Lindal Buchanan, *Rhetorics of Motherhood* (Carbondale: Southern Illinois University, 2013), 8.

28. Buchanan, *Rhetorics of Motherhood*, 8.

29. Buchanan, *Rhetorics of Motherhood*, 8.

30. I.e., breeder, mammy, matriarch, unwed, welfare queen, teen mom, and crack addict mother. See Collins, *Black Feminist Thought*.

31. Harper, "In the Fight of Their Lives"

32. Norman Fairclough, *Language and Power* (Malaysia: Pearson, 2001), 42.

33. Cheryl Glenn, *Unspoken: A Rhetoric of Silence* (Carbondale: Southern Illinois University Press, 2004), 2.

34. Glenn, *Unspoken*, 2.

35. Glenn, *Unspoken*, 21

36. Glenn, *Unspoken*, 25

37. Audre Lorde, "The Transformation of Silence into Language and Action" Paper, Modern Language Association's Lesbian and Literature Panel, Chicago, Illinois, December 28, 1977.

38. Stuart Emmrich, "President Trump Seems to Have a Problem with Yamiche Alcindor. I Wonder Why?," *Vogue.com*, accessed March 31, 2020, https://www.vogue.com/article/yamiche-alcindor-donald-trump-feud.

39. Emmrich, *Vogue.com*.

40. Robin Diangelo, *White Fragility. Why It's So Hard for White People to Talk about Racism* (Boston: Beacon Street Press, 2018), 131.

41. Krista Ratcliff, *Rhetorical Listening* (Carbondale: Southern Illinois University Press, 2005), 17.

42. Tanja Dreher, "Listening Across Difference: Media and Multiculturalism Beyond the Politics of Voice," *Continuum: Journal of Media & Cultural Studies* 23, no. 4 (August 2009): 445–458, 447.

43. Ruha Benjamin, *Race After Technology* (Medford: Polity Press 2019).

44. Dreher, "Listening."

45. bell hooks, *Talking Back: Thinking Feminist, Thinking Black* (New York: Routledge, 2015), chapter 1. Kindle.

Chapter Five

Where Are All the Black Mothers in Pregnancy Books?

In chapters 2, 3, and 4 I describe the negative ethos that Black mothers have as a result of racist discourse and legal policies from the past, and now I want to understand how the ethos and visual image of motherhood reinforce certain ideologies that affect Black maternal health. For this reason, I turn my attention to analyzing the very thing most women buy when they find out they are pregnant—pregnancy books. Pregnancy books belong to the genre of medical writing that prepares women for the physical and emotional changes their body will experience during and after pregnancy. The genre of literature includes brochures, websites, blogs, online videos, pamphlets, and books—which is what I chose to analyze in my study.

I theorize that the medical establishment's poor treatment of Black mothers stems from implicit biases rooted in the bad Black mother trope and the lack of visual representation of Black mothers in what I call the landscape of motherhood. To test this hypothesis, I conducted a critical discourse analysis of popular pregnancy books sold through online retailers Amazon.com and Barnes&Noble.com. In this study, which was conducted in September of 2019, I documented how many books feature a Black woman, child, man, or family on the cover. The only search phrase I used was *pregnancy books*. I only included books that were about pregnancy, postpartum, infertility, nutrition, breast feeding, specific health issues like gestational diabetes, and raising a child during the first year of life. I did not include pregnancy journals, coloring books, or personal memoirs. If the book was a repeat title, I did not count it as part of the total. I did not sort the titles by specific categories such as featured, price, average customer rating, or newest release. I was not interested in the most popular title or books with the best price, rather I was only interested in cover images. Because my search results included thousands of books, I only reviewed the first twenty pages of search results from both sites.

AMAZON.COM CORPUS

My Amazon.com search on the phrase *pregnancy books* gave me twenty thousand titles and from the first twenty pages I reviewed a total of 193 book covers. I noticed there was a mixture of medical pregnancy books with personal memoirs and fun things like coloring books and journals. Out of 193 books 52 feature a White mother on the cover. Two covers show a Black mother, four show a White father and none show a Black father. Thirty-eight covers show White children and two covers depict children from various ethnicities such as Asian and Latino. None of the covers show Black children. Forty-seven covers have written text or non-human pictures (food, environment, hospital). Finally, there were thirty-two books with illustrations of humans. I did not separate them by ethnicity/race, but most of them also showed White women. The complete results are listed below in table 5.1.

BARNES&NOBLE.COM CORPUS

Barnes&Noble.com had a total of 4,720 search results. From that search, I also looked at the first twenty pages for a total of 126 book covers. This website had more pregnancy journals, personal memoirs, and pregnancy erotica than Amazon.com. Out of 120, forty feature White mothers, two feature Black mothers, and one feature a group of multiethnic women. Eleven of the covers feature White children and three feature a group of multiethnic children. Three covers feature White fathers, and none feature Black fathers. Twenty books feature non-human subjects in the form of words or pictures and thirty-three books feature illustrations of humans. The results are listed below in table 5.2.

Analysis of the Data

Critics of my work might suggest that including terms like *obstetric and gynecological health*, *Black women's maternal health*, or *child-bearing* would expand my study, but the average woman doesn't say, "I'm bearing a child," or "I need to find a book about maternal health." Furthermore, critics may suggest that my study is one sided because I did not expand it to include additional phrases like "pregnancy books for Black mothers" or seek out pregnancy literature from physicians' offices that have a have a clientele

Table 5.1. Amazon Search Results Using the Phrase *Pregnancy Books*

Category	#
Mothers	
Black	2
White	52
Woman of color nonblack	0
All ethnicities grouped together	0
Fathers	
Black	0
White	4
Man of color nonblack	0
All ethnicities grouped together	0
Mother and Fathers (Parents)	
Black	1
White	2
Family of color nonblack	0
All ethnicities grouped together	0
Mother and Child	
Black	1
White	11
Woman of color	1
All ethnicities grouped together	0
Children	
Black	0
White	38
Child of color	0
All ethnicities grouped together	2
Words, Illustrations, Inanimate Objects	
Only words or pictures of food/environment/hospital	47
Illustrations of humans (no distinction in ethnicity)	32
Total	193

Table 5.2. Barnes & Noble Search Results Using the Phrase *Pregnancy Books*

Category	#
Mothers	
Black	2
White	40
Woman of color nonblack	0
All ethnicities grouped together	1
Fathers	
Black	0
White	3
Man of color nonblack	0
All ethnicities grouped together	0
Mother and Fathers (Parents)	
Black	1
White	1
Family of color nonblack	0
All ethnicities grouped together	0
Mother and Child	
Black	0
White	7
Woman of color	1
All ethnicities grouped together	3
Children	
Black	0
White	11
Child of color	0
All ethnicities grouped together	3
Words, Illustrations, Inanimate Objects	
Only words or pictures of food/environment/hospital	20
Illustrations of humans (no distinction in ethnicity)	33
Total	126

comprised of women from all ethnic backgrounds primarily. Nor did I attempt to find out what kind of pregnancy literature a Black owned practice might give to patients. Even though maternal health and Black maternal health are a national conversation, which has made these phrases popular when we talk about pregnancy, people's language use has not changed. For example, people still say, "I'm pregnant." "She's pregnant." "We're pregnant," and that is why I choose to focus only on the phrase *pregnancy books*.

Furthermore, I would like to point out that Black mothers see themselves as mothers not *Black mothers*. Nobody walks around saying, "Hey, I'm a Black mom. I have two Black children," but because motherhood is racialized, and White mothers are the center of the landscape of motherhood, society forces racial categorization on our expressions of motherhood. I center Black women and the use of the phrase *pregnancy books* because I am attempting to highlight what I already know to be true: society knowingly racializes motherhood and then feigns ignorance when terms like *Black mother* are used.

My point is not that there isn't material for Black mothers out there. Nor do I believe Black women are demanding pregnancy literature just for themselves or even need it. My point is that Black mothers aren't even invited into the circle of motherhood in a way that would count their experiences as relevant to other mothers. I'm arguing that only White women are used when stylizing the visual of motherhood in America. So, when I consider those critics, I am reminded of the audacity of White privilege that suggests Black people need to make racism easily visible and palatable so that (some, not all) White people will believe it exists; despite the evidence that it exists, because Black women experience it every day. I am also reminded of what Toni Morrison writes about the White gaze and identity when she shared this at Oregon State.

> The very serious function of racism ... is distraction. It keeps you from doing your work. It keeps you explaining, over and over again, your reason for being. Somebody says you have no language and so you spend 20 years proving that you do. Somebody says your head isn't shaped properly so you have scientists working on the fact that it is. Somebody says that you have no art so you dredge that up. Somebody says that you have no kingdoms and so you dredge that up. None of that is necessary.[1]

This gaze also prevents some medical professionals from owning their biases and working to see Black mothers in a different light when providing maternal care.

In total I reviewed 319 book covers and 28.8 percent of the books feature White moms and 1.25 percent feature Black mothers. Additionally, 15.36 percent feature White children, and 0 percent feature Black children. The data in this small sampling indicates the design conventions of pregnancy books promote White mothers and children as the visual standard in pregnancy literature. And I must ask how is it that in 2020 Black mothers only represent 1.25 percent of the visual representation of a small-scale critical discourse analysis of pregnancy books. Why are Black mothers visually erased from pregnancy book covers? Who is responsible for their erasure? Does this erasure affect the maternal health crisis in our country? Because we forget the power of the image and its ability influence our biases and systems of power, I start my analysis with these questions.

WHO ARE THE GATEKEEPERS OF AMERICA'S MATERNAL HEALTH NARRATIVE?

Based on the small sampling from my study, it is clear to me that Black mothers are erased from commercially produced pregnancy books and are not the primary image used on a regular basis. I posit the erasure of Black mothers is an example of what Norman Fairclough describes as the power of cross-cultural discourse to maintain oppressive power structures. This is achieved by controlling and circulating discourse in a given society using cultural gatekeepers.[2] Gatekeepers are typically from the dominate power group and have a vested interest in the "domination of minorities by the White middle class."[3] Although American culture appears on the surface to be one culture, anyone who has lived here knows there are several hyphenated groups that make up the American experience. However, White American culture is the normative culture and all other ethnic groups fall into a hyphenated existence. Hence the need to maintain control of cross-cultural discourses and the cultural memories that support America's ethos. I identify three cultural gatekeepers: medical associations, authors, and book publishers.

In the world of maternal health, gatekeepers come from a variety of places and can include medical associations like the American Board of Obstetrics and Gynecology (ABOG), of course physicians, nurses, midwives, and other professionals such as doulas, lactation consultants, book publishers, and authors. Medical associations control the education and licensing of OBGYNs with their research, conferences, and membership. For example, doctors complete their medical degree, complete a four-year obstetrics and gynecology residency, and may elect to become board certified. In addition to their education and credentialing, some doctors become fellows of the American Congress of Obstetricians and Gynecologists (FACOG) which is also a board certification. Often pregnancy literature and commercially produced books are written by medical professionals who are validated by these organizations, which makes them a gatekeeper for the maternal health field.

Authors, who make up the second group, also share in gatekeeping because they write pregnancy books and other literature from a sanctioned narrative and if they are a medical professional with memberships in these credentialing bodies mentioned above, they are not going to write a book that does not match what is approved by their accrediting bodies and professional organizations. Additionally, maternal health is a field where the reader wants to know that the content has been vetted and the author is credible. This is important for the reader and the publisher because no one wants their reputation tainted by misinformation that potentially harmed a woman or her child. Additionally, authors are going to write what their publisher believes will sell. Even if they feel inclined to present other images and experiences of motherhood, their work might be considered non saleable by the publisher. As a result, any alternative to the White, middle-class experience of motherhood is visually repressed by gatekeepers especially when most publishers have access to thousands of stock images they can choose from for cover art, which brings me to another question—who gets to determine stock images. That's another question for another time.

Publishing houses are gatekeepers because they have final say over a book's content. In some instances, the author may have more control, but what I am suggesting is that gatekeepers will always seek to align with the approved narrative and for the landscape of motherhood it is a White mother, child, or family. The power and authority of those who chose these images and the audience's expectations cannot be downplayed even though pregnancy literature has a diverse audience. I also wonder if publishers feel that White women would not purchase a book with a Black woman on the cover. That is a very real question, because often White people do not see Black people as part of their world in the same way Black people have to see them as part of theirs. To illustrate this point of Whiteness being centered, I turn to a 1998 interview where Toni Morrison was asked by Jana Wendt, a White woman, when she would "incorporate White lives" in a meaningful and substantial way in her literature. I've decided to include the entire exchange because it is often quoted out of context:

> Wendt: You have in your writing certainly marginalized Whites, why are they of no particular interest to you or seemingly no particular interest.
>
> Morrison: Well I was interested in another kind of literature that was not just confrontational. Black versus White. I was really interested in Black readership. I wanted to do, I think, for me the allegory or the parallel is Black music, which is as splendid and complicated and wonderful as it is because its audience was within its primary audience. The fact that it has become universal, worldwide, anyone everyone can play it, and it has evolved is because it wasn't tampered with and editorialized within the community. So I wanted the literature that I wrote to be that way. I could just go straight to where the soil

was, where the fertility was in this landscape and also I wanted to feel free not to have the White gaze in this place that was so precious to me, which is the work.

Wendt: And you will maintain this safe place for yourself, for your art. You don't think you will ever change and write books that incorporate White lives into them substantially?

Morrison: I have.

Wendt: In a substantial way.

Morrison: You can't understand how powerfully racist that question is, can you? You could never ask a White author, "When are you going to write about Black people?" Whether he did or not, or she did or not. Even the inquiry comes from a position of being in the center.

Wendt: And being used to being in the center

Morrison: And being used to being in the center and saying, "Is it ever possible that you will enter the mainstream?" It's inconceivable that where I already am is the mainstream.

Wendt: Oh no that wasn't the implication of my question, I think you are very much in the mainstream. It's a question of the subject of your narrative. Whether you want to alter the parameters of it, whether you see any benefit in doing that or will you clearly see disadvantages in doing it from your own point of view?

Morrison: Artistic disadvantages. There are not pluses for me. Being an African American writer it's sort of like being a Russian writer, who writes about Russia in Russian for Russians and the fact that it gets translated and read by other people is a benefit, it's a plus but he's not obliged to ever consider writing about French people, or Americans, or anybody.

Wendt: When we were talking earlier about being or not being in the mainstream you are sure in the mainstream when it comes to public acclaim

Morrison: I can't tell you how satisfying it is to know that I have earned a readership that is that large—as large as it is. I stood at the border, stood at the edge and claimed it as central, claimed it as central and let the rest of the world move over to where I was.[4]

Morrison's response suggests, as do I, that White people are not ever really forced to center the Black experience; therefore, there is a great possibility that the *White gaze* would prevent White women from believing a pregnancy book with a Black woman on the cover is for her. She might think it is a book only for Black mothers because of how Black mothers are racialized as the *other*.

The erasure of Black mothers has far reaching affects. Because these books are written by medical professionals and are commercially produced, authors and medical professionals disassociate and *other* Black mothers from the positive connotations of motherhood. According to Barton and Barton *Othering* is a process by which those who are in the dominant position in society exclude groups of people by focusing on the concept of privileging. The "rules for inclusion" dictate what cultures are represented and in what order. And in this instance, the inclusion of a considerably higher number of White women imparts privilege to this group because they are the only mothers represented.[5] When Black mothers and mothers of color are not included on the covers of pregnancy books society is encouraged to see White mothers as the defining image for positive representations of motherhood. The lack of representation subconsciously reiterates the stereotypes that good mothers are White and Black mothers not because they do not and cannot fit into the experiences and expectations of White, heterosexual, middleclass women. As such, Black moms are codified in a way that erases them. Their visibility is only necessary when people in power wish to support or revamp existing negative stereotypes to fit political agendas like welfare reform.

In a 2019 survey of 212 Black mothers 64.25 percent reported buying pregnancy literature when given the news they were pregnant and only 6.38 percent reported seeing Black mothers either in photographs or drawn illustrations as part of the book, and 59.04 percent said they did not see any Black mothers represented. From this same group 48.70 percent reported the pregnancy literature they received from their OBGYN did not visually show Black mothers or mothers from various ethnic backgrounds (either in photographs or drawn illustrations) and 18.65 percent said yes, and 32.64 percent said they could not recall. These statistics indicate that Black mothers receive information about pregnancy from a variety of resources, but they are not visually represented in the commercially produced pregnancy books. Reproducing an ideology of White motherhood requires the visual to match the written discourse and unspoken cultural assumptions.

One might argue that women of any ethnicity can sell a pregnancy book, but if that is true then why not include diverse representations of mothers on covers. Why not include images of African American, Latino, Asian, and multiracial mothers on the covers? I want to be clear; I'm not arguing the content of these books do not apply to Black mothers, rather I'm arguing that the visual repression of Black mothers from pregnancy books is an indication of a broader, systemic problem of bias affecting the field of maternal health. The images associated with Black mothers negatively affect how Black motherhood is constructed for public consumption and create a written and visual narrative that demonizes Black mothers and leads to them being dismissed or ignored by medical providers. The dismissal of their concerns causes them to suffer higher rates of complications, subsequently increasing the maternal mortality rate among Black women. In chapter 6, "Reproductive Justice and Black Women's Lives," I discuss how race and class impact Black women's access to contraceptives and abortion services.

NOTES

1. Toni Morrison, "A Humanist View," Portland State University's Oregon Public Speakers Collection: "Black Studies Center Public Dialogue. Pt 2, May 30, 1975.
2. Norman Fairclough, *Language and Power* (Malaysia: Pearson, 2001), 40.
3. Fairclough, *Language*, 40.
4. Toni Morrison, "Toni Morrison Uncensored" interviewed by Jana Wendt, audio, 1998 https://www.youtube.com/watch?v=DQ0mMjII22I.
5. Ben Barton and Martha Lee Barton, "Ideology and the Map: Toward a Postmodern Visual Design Practice, in Central Works in Technical Communication, eds. Johndan Johnson-Eilola and Stuart Selber (New York: Oxford University Press, 2004), 232–251, 252.

Chapter Six

Reproductive Justice and Black Women's Lives

Contraceptives have a long history in America and have always been controlled by men and their perceived understanding of women's sexuality and reproduction. In 1960 the Food and Drug Administration (FDA) approved the first oral contraceptive Enovid. Long-term birth control was made available to women in 1968 with the FDA approval of intrauterine devices (IUDs) like Lippes Loop and Copper 7. The progress of contraceptive use was life changing for women in general, but for Black women the intersection of class and race proved to be a barrier in providing access to *safe* contraceptives. I place emphasis on the word *safe* because so many poor Black women and women of color were used as test subjects for long-acting reversible contraception (LARCs).

Despite the first oral contraceptive (Enovid) being legally available to all women in 1972, regardless of marital status, physician-controlled IUDs like the Dalkon Shield or Depo-Provera appeared to be the physician/government choice for Black women's contraceptives. In her book *Medical Apartheid* Harriet Washington demonstrated that LARCs were touted as a safe way for women to control their reproductive health, but for Black women, again, the conversation was about the *appearance* of control. However, that control was connected to a larger racial and economic agenda. My own view is that LARCs are connected to the images of Black women as breeders and welfare queens. The underlying assumption is that Black women will not control their reproductive capabilities; therefore, physicians and governments suggest LARCs as a solution. As such, women were forced in some cases and strongly encouraged in others to use LARCs. And when they complained of problems their request for removal was ignored, sometimes denied, or they were misdiagnosed with a venereal disease.

One IUD, the Dalkon Shield, proved disastrous. The design of the device predisposed women to pelvic inflammatory disease (PID) and sepsis (blood poisoning) and if left untreated could result in infertility.[1] At least eighteen women died, numerous women reported infections, and many women were sterilized from using the Dalkon Shield. While I do not know the race of the women who died or the number of Black women who suffered from infections, 300,000 women across this nation filed a class action lawsuit against its makers the A.H. Robin Company. Dalkon is representative of what happens when women complain about a contraceptive being unsafe and those in power not responding because women's health is not taken seriously. As a result, a substantial number of women from that time period had full hysterectomies as a result of reoccurring PID caused by the Dalkon Shield. Stories like the Dalkon Shield, Depo-Provera, and Norplant are demonstrative of the little value placed on women's bodies and when that value is applied to Black women—it decreases significantly. As is the case with American medicine,[2] Black women's bodies were, once again, used for unscrupulous medical testing, but this time it was for contraceptives.

In 1978 medical researchers tested Depo-Provera on healthy Black and Native women in an experimental contraceptive study.[3] The FDA denied Depo-Provera as a contraceptive in 1978 and 1983. It was only approved for treatment of endometrial or renal cancer; however, it finally received FDA approval in 1992 on the condition that the manufacturer conduct a post-approval study on the risk of osteoporosis. To this day Depo-Provera still has troubles with its image and product recalls.

Harriet Washington alludes to the problem with physician-controlled contraceptives when she details how poor Back women and girls were targeted for Norplant implantation. Norplant was covered by Medicaid, incentivized by social reform programs, tested in poor communities across the country, and marketed to doctors who treated Black women and teens. To demonstrate how insidious the racialized discourse surrounding Black fertility was during the 1990s politicians and drug companies set their sights on using the Laurence G. Paquin Middle School as a test site for Norplant. Out of the 350 girls attending the school, 345 were Black and these girls, some as young as thirteen, were sometimes forced to have the implantation.[4] To add insult to injury parents did not have the opportunity to consult with their daughters on the matter because parental consent was not a requirement. Those in charge argued it was a privacy issue in order to get around parental involvement. The explicit targeting of Black women and girls and the disregard for parental control over Black children is reminiscent of chattel slavery and the treatment Black women and children received so many years ago. Norplant is yet another example of Black women being used as test subjects and being denied recourse when they experienced side effects. For example, when women started complaining of side effects such as weight gain, acne, mood changes, menstrual changes, and headaches, Medicaid was reluctant to pay the necessary $500.00 needed to remove Norplant. Norplant was eventually recalled in 2000.

For as long as we can remember Black women have struggled against a system that controlled their access to safe contraceptives and abortion. At the turn of the twentieth century the reproductive conversation was about having little to no access to medical care in rural towns and growing northern cities, resisting forced sterilization, and access to safe contraceptive and abortion services. As I have noted in chapter 2 the American government and eugenics proponents used forced sterilization as a form of birth control for poor, Black women. The purported goal was to limit Black women's fecundity as a way to save the government money because there would be less women with children on welfare. In addition to having access to *safe* contraceptives Black women also faced an uphill battle with *Roe v. Wade* because in many ways *Roe* did not provide safe and equitable abortion care for Black women.

WHAT *ROE V. WADE* REALLY MEANT FOR BLACK WOMEN

As I think about women like myself who came of age during the 1990s, it is crystal clear now how little we knew about the risks involved with using Norplant, Depo-Provera, the pill, or even the right for safe abortions. We grew up with *Roe v. Wade* being lauded as a hard won gift to my generation from the pro-choice, feminist movement without having a real understanding of the dangers that women (our mothers, grandmothers, and great-grand mothers) endured under stringent abortion laws; we did not fully understand the nuances of state and federal regulations; nor, did we understand what it meant for Black women whose lives intersected at the crossroads of race, gender, class and motherhood.

Understanding the Historical Dangers of Abortion Laws

For single women pregnancy was a mark of shame. It was an indication she had indulged in sexual intercourse outside of the sanctity of marriage. For married women pregnancy was the mark of her completing her duty to family and country and entering into the coveted role of mother. If she already had children a new pregnancy may have represented fear as she tried to figure out how she would care for another child. If she was single, the fear might sound like, "How will I care for this child at all." When abortion is discussed people often forget the real-life circumstances affecting the women who need an abortion. I believe deeply that abortion is never a simple choice and I am not sure where the narrative that women just randomly wake up and say to themselves "Today is the day. I am having an abortion because I do not want to have this baby" comes from. This erroneous narrative of shame and stigma oversimplifies the complex and difficult choice women face. In the mid-1800s abortion became criminalized in America and by the turn of the nineteenth century it was completely outlawed. As a result, for close to 100 years American women were forced into having botched, back alley abortions where knitting needles, wire hangers and toxic combinations of Lysol and bleach douches (just to name a few) were used to abort a fetus. Consequently, hospital emergency rooms were full of women with infections, uterine hemorrhages and other complications. While it is hard to determine the exact number of women who died from illegal abortions, it is safe to assume that women did in fact die from illegal abortions and some were rendered barren because of the desperate and dangerous choices they made prior to 1973 and the passing of *Roe*.

Abortion and Black Women's Crossroads

As I have stated before class and race are compelling barriers to abortion access for Black women. Researchers at the Guttmacher Institute suggest the struggles of acquiring and managing contraceptive use—issues tied to economics and community can account for one of the reasons Black women followed by Hispanic women consistently have the highest abortion rates in the country.[5] From an economic point of view, a woman who does not have the money to purchase birth control pills has an inconsistent pattern of use with her oral contraceptives. Additionally, if she lacks access to health care or has unstable living conditions (homelessness or living in a shelter) acquiring birth control pills, the patch, or a diaphragm might not be a high priority because she is trying to secure a safe living environment. And if this same woman depends on using a condom, a level of uncertainty is introduced because she has to make sure it was used correctly to prevent conception. If we then add domestic violence, drug use, alcohol abuse, or sex work into the mix these elements further remove women from the ability to use contraceptives regularly and effectively. All of these variables affect contraceptive use and the potential for unintended pregnancies. For some Black women, not all, the reasons listed above are contributing factors for the high numbers of abortions in communities of color. So, *Roe* was and remains an important part of Black women's health needs.

The Guttmacher Institute estimates that before *Roe* 200,000 to 1.2 million illegal abortions per year were performed in the United States.[6] *Roe* gave women the right to select whether to abort a pregnancy based the *right to privacy*; however, the decision was dictated by the gestation of the pregnancy. In the first trimester the decision belonged to the woman. In the second trimester the government had the right to regulate the abortion to protect the mother's health, and in the third trimester the government could prevent the abortion to protect a fetus that was able to survive outside of the womb as long as the mother's health was not in danger. *Roe* was revolutionary in some ways, but it still left Black women in need of safe reproductive care.

Understanding these limitations as a 40-plus-year-old woman in 2020 makes me reconsider the victory because I now recognize that *Roe* only made abortion legal. It did not provide women with unmitigated control over their body or the choice. And it placed poor women and Black women in even greater financial straits due to the Hyde Amendment of 1976 that banned the use of federal funding for abortions. Poor women were subject to government-controlled healthcare programs like Medicaid. Women who worked for government agencies like the military, Peace Corps or federal prisons also faced "discriminatory restrictions on abortion care and funding with federally funded insurance."[7] Over the years the Hyde Amendment has been revised to include rape, incest and maternal health clauses, but little has been done to truly make abortion accessible across class lines. As such poor women have not always benefited from *Roe* in the same way that wealthy women have. If poor women were unable to use federal funding, did not have private insurance, or the money to pay out of pocket for an abortion, they fell victim to the matrix of issues surrounding abortion rights. When poor women are faced with the question of abortion their choice goes beyond the expense. Her choice goes beyond her immediate personal needs because she must consider her resources such as access to childcare, a living wage and the physical environment.

When I consider these intersections, I often wonder about a high school friend who became pregnant in the 7th grade and was sent away to a girl's home for pregnant teens. At the home she was able to continue going to school, put her child for adoption, and return to life with her mother. We never discussed if she ever considered an abortion, but thinking about this story some 30 years later, and all the rumors about girls getting abortions in high school I ask, "How did these girls and their families navigate the financial and gestation constraints of *Roe*?" Was abortion ever a real consideration for these young women given their age and parental finances? For some the question is yes. Pamela Bridgewater Toure's account of her pregnancy and abortion at age 16 is demonstrative of the freedom women had to control their decisions before politicians began chipping away at *Roe*. Toure shares this account in her edited chapter "Transforming Silence" and I have decided to share an excerpt because it illustrates the freedoms of *Roe* that are no longer available for women today (in the year 2020) because of state regulations that continue to erode women's rights.

> I got the yellow pages, turned to abortion, closed my eyes, picked three doctors, and chose the one with the friendliest sounding name. I chose Dr. R. I called his office and got the price for the procedure. He had a sliding scale, $150–210, based on how much I could afford and how far along I was. I made

the appointment for the next week. When the time came, my boyfriend and I went together. . . .

When my name was called, I went into a small room with the nurse practitioner, who explained the procedure in detail. She told me about the risks. She answered my questions and told me that she needed to take a blood sample to confirm that I was pregnant. After the confirmation, she asked me about my family and medical history. Finally, she asked me whether I was sure I did not want to have a baby. I said, "Yes, I'm positive." After signing the consent forms and paying the bill, she took me to meet the doctor. He told me his name and asked me about school and sports. After a short chat about the procedure, he said that he would leave the room and the nurse would help me prepare. He later gave me a shot in the arm and I went to sleep. After the procedure, a nurse led me to another room with a big comfortable chair in which I reclined and went back to sleep, covered by a blanket. When I woke up again, the nurse told me that everything went well and I would be fine. She said the anesthesia might make me nauseous and weepy, and I might have cramps and bleeding. She gave me some orange juice, a cookie, and over the counter pain reliever, a "What to Expect" fact sheet with a number to call if I had any problems, and an extra-long sanitary pad. I dressed myself and went home.[8]

Toure notes that her abortion experience was easy in comparison to what women today endure and uses it as part of class discussions as a way to demonstrate how she arrived at the important choice. The issue of parental consent, waiting periods, funding, and the lack of abortion clinics across the country make it difficult for women to start the process. The fact that Toure was able to manage this process as a 16-year-old and did not have to deal with waiting periods, protestors, counseling services (in my opinion meant to delay a decision) are examples of the constraints *Roe* has suffered over the last 30 years.

As *Roe* continues to change with the whims of politicians and social justice reformers, states continue to revisit and pass new laws to undermine the choice of women—further ostracizing those in need. The Guttmacher Institute reports "that between January 1, 2001 and July 1, 2019, states enacted 483 new abortion restrictions, and these account for nearly 40 percent of all abortion restrictions in the decades since *Roe*."[9] As of today (May 7, 2020) there are limits on physician and hospital requirements, gestation, public funding, partial birth abortion, private insurance coverage, mandated counseling and parental involvement. These major provisions affect women's access across the country. For example, in my home state of North Carolina, there were fourteen abortion clinics in 2017 which is down from the sixteen clinics that were open in 2014. I am not sure if the number continues to decrease, but as of September 1, 2019, patients must receive counseling services and then wait 72 hours before the procedure can be completed. Women on state insurance plans under the Affordable Care Act or public employees can only use their coverage if the mother's life is in danger or if she is a victim of rape or incest. Telemedicine is also prohibited, thus denying women who do not live close to an abortion clinic, hospital, nonspecialized clinic, or doctor's office that performs abortions from accessing the abortion pill. So, out of the 100 counties in North Carolina, women have 14 abortion clinics to choose from and even less options for hospitals and private practice providers. Furthermore, "some 90% of North Carolina counties had no clinics that provided abortions, and 53% of North Carolina women lived in those counties."[10]

North Carolina also prohibits public funding for abortion services unless a woman is a victim of rape or incest or the pregnancy will endanger the mother's life. Minors must have parental consent and ultrasounds confirming a pregnancy must be performed. Additionally, an abortion cannot be performed for the purpose of sex selection. Finally, there are equipment, staff and facility restrictions that pro-choice advocates find burdensome. If these restrictions had been in place when Toure need an abortion, she would have never been able to secure a safe and affordable abortion. And when we consider that her parents knew she was pregnant and that she was clear that she did not want to have a child, the need for counseling could have caused undue stress on the 16-year-old Toure. While it seems that Toure paid cash for her procedure, if she had to use public or private health insurance that would have been another challenge. Even as I research and write this book states are still passing repressive laws. Ohio just passed HB413 which states "A physician who does all of the following is not subject to criminal prosecution, damages in any civil action, for violation of this chapter: (A) Using reasonable medical judgement, believes it is highly probable that the pregnant women will die from a certain fatal condition before her unborn child is viable; (B) Performs a surgery, before the unborn child is viable, for the sole purpose of treating the pregnant woman's fatal condition; (C) Takes all possible steps to preserve the life of the unborn child, while preserving the life of the woman. Such steps include, if applicable, attempting to re-implant an ectopic pregnancy into the woman's uterus."[11] That fact that it is dangerous and scientifically impossible to relocate an ectopic pregnancy from a fallopian tube to a woman's uterus shows the lack of understanding that politicians have of what's physically possible.[12] The politician who wrote the bill is quoted as saying "I heard about it over the years. I never questioned it or gave it a lot of thought."[13] His flip admission shows how little some, not all, policy makers care about the health of women.

To deal with constant changes to the law, pro-choice organizers have experienced a paradigm change in how they understand abortion and the complex moving pieces. There is also a push to build coalitions that on the surface might seem dissimilar but are really fighting for the same thing. As a result, a number of organizations working on behalf of all women but rooted in the experiences of Black women and other women of color have been formed—groups like the Combahee River Collective and organizations that followed such as SisterSong, The National Women's Health Network, Raising Women's Voices, the National Latina Institute for Reproductive Health, the Black women's Health Imperative, the National Asian Pacific American Women's Forum, and Black Mammas Matter Alliance have all lent their unified power to advancing access to reproductive health care services and of course abortion rights. Unlike the pro-life movement where the focus has traditionally been on using voting power to redress issues of abortion rights, grassroots organizations are educating their communities about policies and how they affect their material realities. Today there are also more youth organizations (Third Wave Fund, URGE, Feminist Majority Foundation, and others) engaged in reproductive justice and expanding the discussion to include the needs of the LGBTQ community. Organizations like this show how Black feminist, women of color and LGBTQ communities reconstruct their position from the margins of the feminist movement and move beyond the pro-choice conversation of *Roe v. Wade* to focus on other issues affecting the reproductive lives of women. This kind of work, situated within communities at the ground level, also gave voice to women who wanted more control of the conditions of their birth and the ability to hold the medical establishment accountable.

NOTES

1. Anna Bahr, "As Memories of Dalkon Shield Fade, Women Embrace IUDs Again," *Ms.Magazine*, August 29 2010, https://msmagazine.com/2012/08/29/as-memories-of-dalkon-shield-fade-women-embrace-iuds-again/.
2. Anesthesia free medical examinations on plantations, anatomical displays of Black bodies at fairs and circuses, the Tuskegee experiment, experimentation on Black prisoners, and forced sterilization.
3. Harriet A. Washington, *Medical Apartheid: The Dark History of Medical Experimentation on Black Americans from Colonial Times to the Present* (New York: Anchor Books, 2006), 209.
4. Washington, *Medical Apartheid*.
5. Susan A. Cohen, "Abortion and Women of Color: The Bigger Picture," *The Guttmacher Policy Review* (New York: The Guttmacher Institute, August 6, 2008), 2. https://www.guttmacher.org/gpr/2008/08/abortion-and-women-color-bigger-picture.
6. History.com, "Roe v. Wade is Decided," *This Day in History* (History.com, November 13, 2009), https://www.history.com/topics/womens-rights/roe-v-wade.
7. Marlene Gerber Fried, "Reproductive Rights Activism after Roe," in *Racial Reproductive Justice: Foundations, Theory, Patrice, and Critique*, eds. Loretta J. Ross, Lynn Roberts, Erika Derkas, Whitney Peoples, and Pamela Bridgewater Toure (New York: Feminist Press, 2017), 141.
8. Pamela Bridgewater Toure "Transforming Silence," in *Racial Reproductive Justice: Foundations, Theory, Patrice, and Critique*, eds. Loretta J. Ross, Lynn Roberts, Erika Derkas, Whitney Peoples, and Pamela Bridgewater Toure (New York: Feminist Press, 2017), 237.

9. Guttmacher Institute. "State Facts About Abortion in North Carolina" (New York: Guttmacher Institute, 2017), 2. https://www.guttmacher.org/sites/default/files/factsheet/sfaa-nc_2.pdf.
10. Guttmacher Institute. "State Facts," 2.
11. https://www.legislature.ohio.gov/legislation/legislation-documents?id=GA133-HB-413, accessed. November 29, 2019.
12. The American College of Obstetricians and Gynecologists, "Ectopic Pregnancy, Frequently Asked Questions" (Washington: American College of Obstetricians and Gynecologists), accessed November 29, 2019.
13. Associated Press, "Lawmaker Says He Didn't Research Ectopic Pregnancy Procedure Before Adding to Bill," WOSU Public Media, December 12, 2019. https://radio.wosu.org/post/lawmaker-says-he-didnt-research-ectopic-pregnancy-procedure-adding-bill#stream/0.

Chapter Seven

Black Midwives and Reclaiming Choice

Part of reproductive justice theory advocates for women to have children according to personal preferences. This means they control how they give birth, who assists them with birth, where they give birth, and their techniques for labor. For all women midwifery, which was once a tradition of women's work, eventually became a scapegoat of patriarchal medical professionals and politicians who wanted to control yet another part of women's lives. It was not enough that women's sexuality and their reproductive choices had to be controlled by men, now they wanted to control a woman's labor and delivery too. So when men became interested in obstetrics, giving birth became a pathology that needed to be medicalized, women lost control. This takeover affected *all* women, but for Black women it meant that they would have to deal with the White medical establishment which they already had little trust in.[1] Existing feminist theory and maternal theory have touched on the rift between the medical establishment and midwives, but what I would like to discuss is how race affected that rift and the work of Black midwives. The history of Black midwifery is the history of Black maternal care which developed because of racist isolation—especially in the American south. The culture of Black maternal health was influenced by racism, a struggle for education, training, and access, the contempt obstetrics physicians had for midwives; and a shift in Black consciousness.

THE BEGINNING OF BLACK MIDWIFERY

Medical doctors who were responsible for tending to enslaved women viewed Black midwives as competition. The tensions that existed between midwives and doctors was situated in the doctor's need to earn a living. So, when midwives administered care for slaves, their economic wellbeing was threatened. White doctors did not necessarily want to deliver enslaved children, yet they did not want Black midwives and healers to outdo them in ability and competence. Rather they wanted to supervise Black midwives. White doctors complained about Black midwives' lack of formal training and education. However, Washington argues most White doctors, at the time, had no more than a high school education and a few years of medical school education.[2] Before medical schools opened their doors, most doctors worked in the apprenticeship system. Flexner in his 1910 article *Medical Education in America rethinking the Training of American Doctors*, describes a system where young men "ran his master's errands, washed bottles, mixed the drugs, spread the plasters, and finally, as the stipulated term drew toward its close, actually took part in the daily practice of his preceptor."[3] Most of these doctors learned how to deliver children and the intricacies of female reproductive organs because of their work in slave quarters, which is the same training midwives received. White doctors also disliked midwives because it was believed they assisted with abortions. Despite their dislike for attending births, doctors still saw maternal care as a steady form of income and an opportunity to practice delivering babies. And because of the income opportunity antebellum physicians played on slaveholders' need for having healthy women for breeding. Therefore, doctors advertised their ability to cure infertility, menstrual, and uterine problems.

The obsession with the reproductive abilities of enslaved women put them at risk for dangerous medical interventions. Slave culture was oppositional to a healthy pregnancy. Pregnant women were subjected to heavy workloads, extreme heat and cold, and physical abuse. Enslaved women who worked the fields paid a high price in unrealistic work regimens. The strenuous work and long hours were detrimental to having a healthy pregnancy. Some southern doctors suspected the extreme work load contributed to spontaneous abortions in women rather than women secretly trying to abort pregnancies, yet southern doctors continued to support a culture of suspicion concerning miscarriage and infertility by shifting focus from the harsh living conditions pregnant women endured to willful attempts of sabotage—often assumed to be assisted by a granny midwife.

If a mother was lucky enough to carry a child to term, she faced obstacles such as a long labor, the use of ergot or forceps, dangerous caesarean sections, and possible infection at the hands of ill-equipped doctors. Because labor was a process that did not always progress in a timely manner, some women were in labor for as long as four days and others 12 to 16 hours. While labor times vary, even by today's standards, birth is always the same. Labor and birth have three phases. Phase 1 is split into two stages: early and active. In early labor a woman begins to feel mild contractions and her cervix dilates, effaces and begins to soften. During this time a woman might also lose the mucus plug that blocks the cervix's opening. In active labor contractions become increasingly stronger as the cervix dilates. Typically, the cervix dilates about one centimeter per hour and while this is not always the case active labor can last about eight hours or more. The final stage of active labor is called transition, and this is where contractions are their strongest and the cervix has dilated to 10 centimeters. Once the transition ends a woman enters into the second phase of labor which is birth. Contractions, force of the uterus, and active pushing by the woman all work to move the baby down the birth canal. Eventually the child is delivered, and the third stage of birth begins with the delivery of the placenta. During this phase the uterus contracts and with a few additional pushes the placenta is expelled. The process I have described is no different from what was expected to happen during enslaved births; however, the lack of adequate knowledge, insistence on complication free deliveries, and the inability to see Black mothers as human created an environment that was dangerous for both the mother and child.

Medical research is replete with stories of women laboring for days and complications arising, but what research does not fully articulate, although Schwartz alludes to in her work, is the distrust enslaved mothers had for White slaveholders' physicians. Most women preferred a midwife deliver their child. Black midwives, sometimes called granny midwives, were enslaved women who were experienced in delivering babies and had a sort of spiritual quality to them. Typically, Black midwives were trained by another midwife who might be their mother or grandmother and sometimes they were the apprentices to White doctors. Regardless of how she entered the profession, "to be accepted in the slave quarter, a woman had to gain the confidence of other slaves by demonstrating an aptitude or calling. A woman who did not have the support of her people would not have attempted to assist in childbirth."[4] Having a calling also meant having a knowledge of natural remedies, herbs, and roots that could assist with a variety of women's health issues. Black midwives used cotton root to induce labor, calamus root to ease childbirth pains, horsemint leaves to aid in the return of menstruation and other roots such as "red shank, cherry bark, dog-wood bark, prickly-ash roots, bamboo roots, and blackhaw roots."[5]

In addition to their knowledge of herbal remedies they understood the life and death consequences of childbirth and had an astute understanding of the spiritual and scared nature of childbirth. Midwives knew the birth traditions and rituals of African ancestors, and because of this they were able to perform these rites (often in secret) for the wellbeing of the child and mother. For example, African tradition believed that children born en caul (fully enclosed in the amniotic sac) were gifted with second sight into the spiritual world. An en caul birth required special attention and slave holders' physicians did not understand the importance of the caul or even disposing of the placenta appropriately, which also carried special significance in African culture.⁶ Because Black midwives saw enslaved women's humanity, they explained to these mothers what they were experiencing—unlike White physicians who did not think an explanation was owed to them. What many slaveholders and antebellum doctors failed to understand is that the conditions of slavery prevented enslaved women from conceiving, delivering and raising children.

Racism and the Culture of Black Midwifery

Black women have always received poor maternal care in America and by stating this I do not discredit the hard work of Black midwives who delivered babies and administered pre and post-natal care to women. I am talking about the racial caste system that prevented Black midwives, doctors, and patients from having full access to the same resources as White citizens, so midwives were a godsend to Black communities and they were the backbone of both the public health and Black maternal health culture. A starting point for understanding Black women's struggle with the right to choose her birth condition begins with the culture of American midwifery and the tension that existed between White physicians and all midwives. Prior to 1921 midwifery was not regulated and during that time birth was still understood as a natural process and not a pathology. Pregnancy was a part of God's plan. Midwife Onnie Lee Logan supports this notion when she said, "Childbirth is not a sickness—God gonna take care of that."⁷ However, all that changed when the federal government passed the Sheppard-Towner Maternity and Infancy Act in 1921. This policy gave states federal funding to create programs aimed at decreasing the infant mortality and maternal mortality rate. According to Lay, "Fourteen of the states decided that licensing, supervision, and instructing midwives would be their priority. Other states set up infant welfare centers, trained public health nurses, supported home visits by nurses and created prenatal clinics."⁸ The Sheppard-Towner ct Act led to the "establishment of nearly 3,000 prenatal care clinics, 180,000 infant care seminars, and over three million home visits by traveling nurses, and a national distribution of educational literature between 1921 and 1928."⁹ The Act also required lay midwives to become licensed, undergo a physical exam and participate in annual trainings to maintain licensure. Across the nation and particularly in the poor south, Black midwives received training on hygiene and asepsis, prenatal care, and puerperal infection.

Staying the Course Despite Contempt

Under the guise of licensure supervision White doctors and nurses used their interaction with Black midwives to paint a picture of inadequacy—similar to chattel slavery. Despite positive reviews from White staff, their commitment to learning, and the seriousness with which they took their responsibility midwives—particularly Black midwives—were still blamed for maternal and infant deaths. Those in charge of the training programs viewed them as uneducated, dirty, and "far below the European midwife in intelligence and no training under the sun could make a competent obstetric attendant."[10] However, this assertion is unfair because these women worked in some of the poorest parts of America with access to very little resources and in truth they were responsible for changing some of the problems with public health in Black communities. Black maternal health and infant mortality concerns were part of a larger public health crisis in African-American communities which was exacerbated by impoverished living conditions, poor wages, the fear of being used and tricked by White doctors, and the lack of access to medical facilities available for Black patients. These segregated communities did not have anyone else to depend on in regard to health care and these midwives used the Sheppard-Towner Act trainings to ensure their communities benefited from the little bit of medical assistance they could get for them.

Midwives out on visits would report illnesses, check on families, cook for the mother, sew clothes sometimes, and work to get access and resources into these communities to help stave off some of these public health issues. Researchers suggest that because of lay midwives' training in public health and the nurse midwives who followed their path, blindness in children decreased because the midwives would put two drops of silver nitrate in the eyes of the child.[11] Physicians who ran health centers also reported an increase in illness awareness that led Black families to seek treatment before advanced stages of sickness—another result of midwives and their public health outreach in Black communities. Despite all the positive results of the Shepphard-Towner Act and Black midwives training, the success was stymied because of access to additional resources.

Access to Hospitals

At the turn of the twentieth century, Black women had no expectation of maternal care outside of what a midwife would provide.[12] According to Onnie Lee Logan, a lay midwife in Mobile, Alabama "she did not remember a single incidence where a White doctor delivered a Black baby in the home of the mother."[13] Where Black doctors were scarce and White doctors refused to see Black patients, this isolation allowed Black midwives to serve generations of Black families and create a maternal culture of care. And it is ironic that the isolation of the slave quarters and later segregation in southern towns and northern cities is what allowed Black women to have someone they trusted (a midwife) deliver their children.[14] Only if there was a serious medical concern a doctor was called, but by and large midwives did all the work. However, if a mother was seen by a Black physician there was no guarantee she would have access to a medical facility because Black doctors did not have admitting privileges at White hospitals and Black hospitals were few and far between. If she was seen by a White physician, the same rules applied. Black women were not allowed in White hospitals unless there was a colored wing.

Access to a hospital was an ongoing problem across the country and America's racial caste system was detrimental for mothers who had an emergency and needed more than a midwife. For example, Luke acknowledges that some midwives in Alabama and Virginia recalled driving anywhere from 70 to 170 miles to reach a hospital that accepted Black patients.[15] In North Carolina there were only nine hospitals across the state that accepted Black patients, and this was in 1960.[16] "In sixteen southern states, 9.7 million African Americans were served by only seventy-nine Black hospitals, many of which were unaccredited, underequipped, and struggling to stay open under the financial constraints of serving an economically deprived community."[17] Having to drive long distances or simply accept that medical treatment in a hospital was not an option is an example of the intersection of race and motherhood. Eventually federally funded hospitals across the country were forced to desegregate and allow Black physicians and patients entry thanks to cases like Simkins v. Moses H. Cone.[18] However, this did nothing to curb the racist attitudes of White nurses and doctors. The condescending and harsh treatment from White physicians and nurses did not result in what one would call maternal *care*. Onnie Logan recalls that most Black people did not trust White doctors anyway and that the lack of trust came from the dehumanizing treatment they received.[19] However, this started to change slowly once Black midwives started participating in training classes and were able to further their education and work in some hospitals.[20]

Even when nurse midwives started replacing lay midwives, also called direct entry midwives, access to training and professional development eluded Black nurse midwives and physicians. In addition to the lack of education opportunities for medical staff, physicians often had a hard time sustaining a practice because of segregation and the inability of patients to pay. Once federal and state governments began to regulate the profession, midwives struggled to coexist with obstetrics doctors who were members of large associations like the American Medical Association. Ultimately these organizations lobbied politicians for greater restrictions which resulted in midwifery being outlawed across the country. One reason why politicians and medical governing bodies were so successful at outlawing midwifery is because of the ethos they created and used to discuss the skills and education level of the women who practiced. Because of these challenges the culture of Black midwifery changed along with a growing access to public health facilities like health clinics and hospitals. As such there was a shift in the consciousness of Black women in regard to their maternal health.

A Shift in Black Consciousness

The change in Black maternal culture was affected by an increase in federal funding, Medicaid regulations that did not pay for midwifery services, and loosened hospital guidelines allowing Black women to give birth in a hospital. These changes pushed more Black women into hospital births, and many preferred this option. Black women began to view hospital birth as acceptance into American society and a status symbol—an indication that one was upwardly mobile. As more women preferred hospital settings for birth, midwifery and health clinics increasingly became associated with the poor and Black women. Eventually Black doctors began to adopt the attitude of White physicians and felt that midwifery was a necessary evil and advocated for hospital delivery. Although Black women were now able to have hospital births, the racist attitudes prevailed.

White doctors and nurses were condescending, impatient, and rough. Similar to what mothers report today, White doctors believed Black women could withstand pain and were indifferent to their needs. Some women reported forgoing prenatal care because of the rude and uncaring attitudes of physicians. Once admitted to a hospital, mothers were often left to labor alone. White doctors and nurses attributed the cries of pain as animalistic stereotypes and refused to provide medication. This modern way of giving birth was antithetical to what midwives knew to be true—that motherhood and definitely birth was communal in nature and was not meant to happen alone. The loss of midwives affected the Black community in more ways than one, but as the culture changed and Black midwives stopped practicing there was a resurgence of midwifery among wealthy White women and communal living groups who wanted to have home births. As a result, midwifery became associated with White women and the same arguments about regulation, education and direct entry versus nurse midwives resurfaced, but this time Black women did not have the same presence as before.

Today Black women who want to have a home birth or use a midwife face a different set of challenges such as locating a midwife of color, community attitudes, and health insurance. Often Black midwives are hard to find. Even with professional associations and informal networks focused on the needs of Black women, it is still hard to find a Black midwife especially in small rural towns. For instance, when I searched for Black midwives in North Carolina on the site www.sistamidwife.com, my search returned thirty-two professionals. From those 32 women listed, five are listed as midwives and one is listed as a lactation consultant. As of July 1, 2018 North Carolina, has a population of 10,383, 620 people and 22.2 percent of those people identify as Black or African American. So, this means for the entire state of North Carolina there are 5 midwives and 26 doulas[21] as maternal healthcare providers. The number of midwives practicing in North Carolina might be higher, because there is a possibility that some midwives are not part of the site I visited even though they can be listed for free on the website. Even with this preliminary research, my point is confirmed. Black midwives are not plentiful. According to Keisha Goode "black women currently represent less than 2% of the nation's reported 15,000 midwives,"[22] but there is cause for hope as more Black women are entering the midwife profession.

In addition to finding a midwife, overcoming the stigma associated with homebirths and midwives is now a challenge in the Black community. What was once the cornerstone of maternal health is now viewed as inadequate and foreign. I know from my own birth experience when I expressed the desire to perhaps have a midwife assisted homebirth, my friends and family—particularly my mother—thought I had lost my mind. She was worried that I would actually find someone to deliver my child at home. Her reluctance, despite the fact that she and her four siblings were delivered by a midwife at home, made me reconsider my desire. Because of my mother's reaction and the reactions of others I realized that discussing the naturalness of labor and the desire for a midwife was stigmatized. If a woman wants to use a midwife or have a home birth there's a stereotype that only hippies or people who want to live outside of society's norms have home births, or that you are taking unnecessary risks by desiring an alternative to a hospital setting. The mother is left trying to convince their families and friends that home births, water births, or midwife assisted births are safe and acceptable. The irony is that the birth trauma people fear will happen while at home or with a midwife actually happens in hospitals with obstetrics doctors. In my qualitative study "Only White Women Get Pregnant" 39.02 percent of the respondents reported needing an emergency C-section and the reasons run the gamut. For a complete list of the responses to this question, see appendix A.

Today, nurse midwives are more common than we think and private OBGYN practices across the country employ them as part of their pregnancy services. Even though I did not have a home birth, I did have a nurse midwife assisted, hospital birth that almost cost me my life. My second child was also delivered by nurse midwife who was part of a private practice, which leads me to my third point regarding health insurance and the quality of care poor women receive. When I found out I was pregnant with my first child, Naeemah, I was originally part of a private practice and with private insurance. After my initial prenatal visit, I decided I wanted a Black doctor to care for me. I could not envision my current physician delivering my child. Visiting her once a year for a pap smear was one thing but visiting her monthly for prenatal care was another. She was not a bad doctor, but she did not resonate with me. I figured that I would look for a new doctor while I continued to see my current OBGYN. Unbeknownst to me, in this town, doctors did not like to take new patients if you were already part of a practice. In addition to that problem, the Black physician's office that I did find was not accepting new patients, and I was turned away from another popular practice. Knowing I needed to have prenatal care, I decided to continue with the local health clinic until I found a new doctor. I never did. In that clinic setting I found a Black nurse midwife that I absolutely loved and a White one that I liked a lot, and so I decided to stay with the clinic because of the prenatal care I received from the Black woman. What I did not understand was that all the patients were seen by the physicians and nurse midwives, so that anyone of them could deliver your child. I incorrectly assumed that the Black midwife that I felt the most comfortable with would be the one who delivered my child. I did not think to inquire about the doctor's opinion regarding natural birth and induction. And I never thought the negative attitudes from society about Black women would follow me into the labor and delivery world. I was so naive and uninformed.

Because I decided to stay with this health clinic, I witnessed the treatment poor women, regardless of color, received. I witnessed the contempt that was shown to young pregnant women, mothers who already had children and were pregnant again, and immigrant mothers. Most of the women there were uninsured, on Medicaid, underemployed, and of color. There was an attitude of dismissiveness with some of the health care providers and the office staff were sometimes rude. In my last visit before my induction I found out the nurse midwife I really connected with would not be on duty to deliver my baby. The day I was admitted to the hospital for induction, I kept having a bad feeling that I shouldn't show up. I wanted to wait another week and see if the baby would come on her own, but I did not have the courage to say this or a doula to speak on my behalf. I was scared that if I did not follow the medical advice that I was given I would hurt my child. I felt like I needed to follow the plan and be induced. In hindsight I can see now that even though I liked my nurse midwife, I still did not feel comfortable discussing what I envisioned for my labor and delivery with her.

The day I was scheduled to deliver, I was surprised when we started the process. The nurse midwife who started my induction did not explain anything to me. I was hooked up to all these machines and was effectively tethered to the bed by monitoring devices. All the things I had learned in Lamaze class and read about went out the door. I was not there to labor. I was there to be put into labor. The Pitocin drip brought the onset of contractions that I could not bear. The whole experience was traumatic and as I recall the details I still think my nurse midwife was conditioned to treat Black women (the majority of the patients she treated) with disregard. And then there's the element of when you have done something so many times, you expect it to happen the same way every time—hence treating the body as a machine. I do not think she even considered my labor as a unique experience because she too was part of an industrialized view of pregnancy, where the body must operate efficiently.

In the end my education, insurance, and social economic status did not give me agency. I was still a Black woman. I also believe that the poor treatment I received from hospital staff during my first birth stemmed from the fact that I was a patient of the local health clinic which many of the White hospital staff associated with poor, unwed Black women. When I requested a private room, I was told it was not possible. However, after it was discovered I had private insurance through the University of Georgia system I was told that I would have a private room if one was available. I was in the hospital for a week after giving birth—in a private room I should add—and my total bill was close to $30,000.

After giving birth I was rushed into the ER so the attending physician could repair the cervical lacerations I got during labor. I must admit the care I received by staff after my surgery was much better than what I received in labor and delivery. The nurses were nicer and seemed less annoyed when I needed something. I spent two days in the intensive care unit after my surgery and then another three days in a regular hospital room. I also have a sneaking suspicion that I was the talk of the labor and delivery unit, because every time the nurses changed shifts and I met a new nurse, there was this element of surprise when they realized who I was. I remember when I took my first shower after giving birth, I cried and thanked God that I did not die. The experience traumatized me—and this was in a hospital with a nurse midwife and an attending physician. I often wonder if things would have been different if I had a home birth and labored naturally and was not induced.

By the time I was pregnant with my second child, I was part of a private practice again and had a phenomenal certified nurse midwife and supervising OBGY that I trusted—both of whom happened to be White. I mention their Whiteness because it is important to my story as a Black woman. My desire to connect with a Black physician during one of the most vulnerable moments in my life is what drove me to leave my first OBGYN practice. And although I found the care I was looking for the second time around in a private practice, I still would have preferred a Black physician. Living in this small southern town limited my ability to have maternal care options with Black physicians. It was impossible to find any postpartum depression groups too. In any event, my new nurse midwife guided me through my pregnancy and was there to deliver my baby boy. I had to be induced, but because of my first trauma, I was scared. However, this time I was prepared. Everything was explained to me as I progressed and I knew and understood the steps that were happening. I delivered a 9lb baby boy without any incident and went home two days later. The treatment I received from hospital staff was totally different and I believe it was because I was part of a private medical practice that did not have Medicaid patients. My entire experience was different. This story is representative of the stigma that poor women face, and the geographical challenges of finding access to health care providers that a woman can feel comfortable with.

Finding maternal health care and support systems for Black women is becoming easier thanks to a broad network of organizations dedicated to providing Black mothers and other women of color with resources to meet their unique needs. Organizations like BlackMammasMatter, SisterSong, Why Black Babies, Unbuntu Black Family Wellness Collective, The Birthing Place are all resources that were created to meet the needs of Black women. In addition to these spaces Black women are using the internet to circumvent traditionally, approved maternal health gatekeepers. They are sharing birth stories, connecting each other to resources, building communities on social media, and creating and sharing what I like to call maternal health technical communication as a means for efficacy and change. Because technology allows us to share with the world, Black mothers are returning to a natural model of care regarding birth. However, this is not met without challenges, but with the current attention on Black maternal health, hopefully progress will continue. The right to have children under the conditions we choose has many obstacles that Black women have to navigate and once we do give birth the next challenge is actually raising our children in a society that is anti-Black. In chapter 8, I will discuss the challenges associated with hyper surveillance in our communities and how that affects Black mothers and children.

NOTES

1. Jaqueline Wiltshire, Jeroan J. Allison, Roger Brown, and Keith Elder. "African American Women Perceptions of Physician Trustworthiness: A Factorial Survey Analysis of Physician Race, Gender, and Age," *AIMS Public Health* 5, no. 2 (May 17, 2018): 122–134.
2. Harriet A. Washington, *Medical Apartheid: The Dark History of Medical Experimentation on Black Americans from Colonial Times to the Present* (New York: Anchor Books, 2006), 38.
3. Abraham Flexner, "Medical Education in American. Rethinking the Training of American Doctors," *The Atlantic*, June 1910, https://www.theatlantic.com/magazine/archive/1910/06/medical-education-in-america/306088/.
4. Marie J. Schwartz, *Birthing a Slave: Motherhood and Medicine in the Antebellum South* (London: Harvard University Press, 2009), 147.
5. Schwartz, *Birthing*, 150.
6. Schwartz, *Birthing*, 147.
7. Jenny M. Luke, *Delivered by Midwives. African American Midwifery in the Twentieth Century South* (Jackson: The University Press of Mississippi, 2018), 47.
8. Mary Lay. *The Rhetoric of Midwifery, Gender, Knowledge and Power* (New Brunswick: Rutgers University Press, 2002), 65.
9. Katherine Madgett, "Sheppard-Towner Maternity and Infancy Protection Act (1921)." *Embryo Project Encyclopedia*, May 18 2019,http://embryo.asu.edu/handle/10776/11503.
10. Luke, *Delivered*, 234.
11. Luke, *Delivered*.
12. Luke, *Delivered*, 13.
13. Luke, *Delivered*.

14. Luke, *Delivered*, 102–104.
15. Luke, *Delivered*, 59.
16. Jonathan Martin, "Simkins v. Cone (1963)," *North Carolina History Project*, accessed November 20, 2019, https://northcarolinahistory.org/encyclopedia/simkins-v-cone-1963/.
17. Luke, *Delivered*, 102.
18. Karen Kruse, "Simkins v. Cone," *Encyclopedia of North Carolina*, Chapel Hill: University of North Carolina Press, 2006, https://www.ncpedia.org/simkins-v-cone.
19. Luke, *Delivered*.
20. Katherine Madgett, "Sheppard-Towner Maternity and Infancy Protection Act (1921)." *Embryo Project Encyclopedia*, May 18 2019, http://embryo.asu.edu/handle/10776/11503.
21. Doulas provide emotional, physical, and educational support for pregnant women during and after their pregnancy. They are not allowed to deliver a child and are advocates for women when they enter into the birth setting. They are there to ensure that the mother understands what is happening and they are there to ensure that her needs are being met while she labors.
22. Keisha L. Goode, "Birthing, Blackness, and the Body: Black Midwives and Experiential Continuities of Institutional Racism" (PhD diss., City University of New York, 2014), 1–215.

Chapter Eight

The Will to Resist Is a Form of Love

Motherhood as a site of resistance is a theme that feminist and maternal theory scholars have used when describing what it means to raise children in a racially polarized society. Most Black mothers know that their mothering is part love, joy, fear, and resistance. Audre Lorde writes of motherhood,

> raising Black children—female and male—in the mouth of a racist, sexist, suicidal dragon is perilous and chancy. If they cannot love and resist at the same time, they will probably not survive. And in order to survive they must let go. This is what mothers teach—love, survival—that is, self-definition and letting go.[1]

bell hooks writes,

> Black women resisted by making homes where all Black people could strive to be subjects, not objects, where we could be affirmed in our mind and hearts despite poverty, hardship and deprivation, where we could restore to ourselves the dignity denied us on the outside in the public world.[2]

This resistance we speak of is required for teaching Black children how to live in a society where White women and children benefit from the protections of White privilege, and leaves Black families at the mercy of a system that does not value Black bodies, criminalizes the poor, and prevents poor people from access to systems of redress—this is something that Black people know intuitively. It is something that becomes evident as one continues to grow and live in America.

Reproductive justice theory is a strategy for redressing human rights issues that impede families from raising their children in life affirming environments and it is often overlooked in the larger discussion of the pro-choice movement.³ Having the right to raise children means that parents need access to jobs that pay a living wage, access to affordable housing, access to clean, pollution free physical environments, access to education and health care, and access to violence free encounters with police and other non-Black citizens. All of these things work together on behalf of the family unit—no matter the structure, and to fight for these rights is to resist the table scraps America throws at Black and Brown communities. In this chapter I will discuss the systemic structures associated with over policing and inadequate schools because these sites of oppression are starting points for Black and White children's socialization in America.

RESISTING THE SCHOOL TO PRISON PIPELINE

When I consider the challenges facing mothers today, I have to remind myself that there's never been a time in American history where Black bodies were *NOT* under siege. The violence of chattel slavery and segregation remains unmatched in American history, but the covert racism that lingers in our systems of business, government, law enforcement, and education is just as detrimental to the development of Black children as the violence our ancestors endured. Everyday Black mothers find themselves preparing their children for a world that does not acknowledge their humanity and demands their children remain invisible.

One concern for Black parents that does not ring true for White parents is the goal of preparing our children how to deal with and hopefully survive police interactions at school and in the public. The ultimate goal is to ensure that our children make it home and stay clear of the criminal justice system, which has become increasingly harder because of the school-to-prison pipeline. The pipeline is a reference to the large number of minors from poor communities of color who are suspended, pushed out of the education system, and eventually incarcerated due to stringent, zero-tolerance school policies across the nation. Educators note that implicit bias and school resource officers (police in schools) are contributing factors to the school to prison pipeline.⁴ According to the ACLU, "'Zero-tolerance' policies criminalize minor infractions of school rules, while cops in school lead to students being criminalized for behavior that should be handled inside the school."⁵ When students are suspended or expelled they have a higher chance of ending up on the streets, involved in the juvenile justice system, or migrating into the adult penal system. The data is alarming. According to PrisonPolicy.org, everyday "48,000 youth⁶ in the United States are confined in facilities away from home as a result of juvenile justice or criminal justice involvement."⁷ Black children make up a large percentage of youth involved in the juvenile justice system (42 percent of Black boys and 35 percent of Black girls).[8] Wendy Sawyer of Prison Policy.org also finds that a big part of the problem stems from youth being detained for low-level offences. This cycle ends up robbing Black children of "opportunities for education, future employment and participating in our democracy."[9]

Although the numbers of suspensions and expulsions have declined across the nation, students of color are still disproportionally represented. "Black high school students are still twice as likely (12.8 percent) to be suspended as White (6.1 percent) or Hispanic (6.3 percent) high school students"[10] and youth of color, students with disabilities, and LGBTQ students are punished more harshly and more often than their peers for the same behavior.[11] According to attorney Candice Petty,

> Black students are disproportionately suspended from class, starting as early as preschool. Black preschool children are 3.6 times more likely than white children to receive one or more out-of-school suspensions. This pattern continues in K–12 where black students are 1.9 times more likely than white students to be expelled and 2.3 times more likely to be disciplined through involvement of officers, such as a school related arrest. Black girls are 5.5 times more likely to be suspended from school than their white peers. Black girls are more often punished for challenging what society considers "feminine" behavior—things like being candid or assertive, talking back to teachers, as well as less severe transgressions, including chewing gum and dress code violations. Children as young as 5 or 6 years old have been handcuffed in schools and even arrested. The children subjected to this kind of harsh treatment are almost always children of color.[12]

When schools lack the resources needed for effective classroom instruction and teachers are burdened with overcrowded classrooms, many school districts in poor areas respond with zero tolerance polices rather than an increase in the resources needed to educate. The under investment of resources needed to help educators deal with the challenges students bring to class has resulted in the removal of counselors, social workers and mental health professionals in favor of armed, school resource officers who are there to implement zero tolerance policies—and might I add are ill-trained for dealing with children and young adults.

The United States' investment in incarceration and not education is evident in the amount of money spent on the two. Across the country the numbers vary, but on average states spend more on inmates than education. Table 8.1 shows how much money states spent in 2016 on education in comparison to what they spent on the penal system.

I use California and New York because they represent two of the most diverse populations in our country, but southern states like North Carolina, South Carolina, Florida, and Louisiana don't fare much better. These numbers confirm that education is not a priority in America. Because the prison

Table 8.1. Education versus Prison Spending

State	Inmate	Student	Difference
North Carolina	$30,180	$8,792	$21,388
South Carolina	$20,053	$10,249	$9,804
California	$64,642	$11,495	$53,146
New York	$69,355	$22,366	$46,989
Louisiana	$38,296	$11,038	$27,258
Florida	$19,069	$8,920	$10,149

population continues to grow both adults and juveniles states have built more prisons than schools. For example, at the post-secondary level California has built over 20 prisons since 1980 and one university since.[13]

The privatization of the prison industry along with laws targeting poor and Black communities have created a system Michele Alexander defines as the new Jim Crow. Alexander argues that the penal system in the United States has created a caste system that bars people from moving up and accessing resources when she states,

> What is completely missed in the rare public debates today about the plight of African Americans is that a huge percentage of them are not free to move up at all. It is not just that they lack opportunity, attend poor schools, or are plagued by poverty. They are barred by law from doing so. And the major institutions with which they come into contact are designed to prevent their mobility. To put the matter starkly: They current system operates through our criminal justice institutions, but it functions more like a caste system than a system of crime control. Viewed from this perspective, the so called under class is better understood as an *undercaste*—a lower caste of individuals who are permanently barred by law and custom from mainstream society. Although this new system of racialized social control purports to be colorblind, it creates and maintains racial hierarchy much as earlier systems of control did. Like Jim Crow (and slavery), mass incarceration operates as a tightly networked system of laws, policies, customs, and institutions that operate collectively to ensure the subordinate status of a group defined largely by race.[14]

From an early stage in their lives Black children are set up to enter into the penal system via school disruption and once they end up in the juvenile court, the court system works to secure their position in America's underclass.

Due to the unbalanced criminal justice system, the United States has the highest incarceration rate in the world. It's become common to dismiss the parenting concerns of Black parents or suggest that if they were teaching their children deference when dealing with authority, White people, or the police, then Black kids would be safe. But, when we consider Alexander's theory about the new Jim Crow and the number of Black children who are forced into the school-to-prison pipeline because of suspension and expulsion, then we can see how mothering Black children is further exacerbated by the United States' criminal justice system and the use of excessive force.

Excessive force resulting in the deaths of Black men, women, and children are constant stories in daily news feeds. The standard way of thinking about Black lives, although many White Americans will deny this, suggests that Black lives are expendable if they show the proper amount of deference for White America's oppressive institutions. Deference is expected of any Black person regardless of class. For example, Colin Kaepernick's football career ended because he refused to stand for the National Anthem and *took a knee* in protest against the killing of unarmed Black citizens. Kaepernick believes, as do I, that the NFL colluded to keep him out of the league as punishment for taking a political stance. NBA superstar LeBron James was told to "shut up and dribble" by conservative Fox News host Laura Ingraham when he discussed politics in an interview. She suggested that someone who makes $100 million does not have the right to talk about politics; however, what I believe she really meant is that a Black man who makes $100 million should keep his mouth shut, because his point of view is not wanted or valid—only White millionaires can talk about politics in America.

These attitudes silence Black people and contribute to the over policing that happens in our country. Over policing happens in two ways; in White spaces that are not designed for us and in Black communities where we are rendered invisible or hyper visible. It is that invisibility or hyper visibility that is dangerous.[15] "Invisibility makes a person an interloper in spaces that are perceived as off limits and hyper visibility makes a person more visible; therefore, their every action is watched—even when doing the most mundane things."[16]

RESISTING WHITE CITIZEN POLICE

When Black people trespass into spaces that are not designed for them, run of the mill *White citizen police*[17] take on the role of gatekeeper which often ends with police interaction and or physical violence. Consequently, Black mothers are forced to prepare their children for dealing with unwarranted attention from White citizens who see their presence as an affront to the spaces they occupy based on their "presumed superiority."[18] I argue that race is the motivating factor when White citizen police become involved in the basic, daily interactions of Black people because they "feel that they can initiate actions, direct unilateral operations, and control over blacks, who they are told over and over are unthinking, physical creatures dependent and available for entertainment, gratification, and exploitation."[19] For example seventeen year old Trayvon Martin was followed and shot while walking home from a convenience store, and seventeen year old Jordan Davis was shot for playing his music too loud in a parking lot. The most recent example of White citizen police killing a Black man is the murder of Ahmaud Arbery who was targeted, followed and confronted by two White men in Brunswick, Georgia while jogging. White citizen police are a danger to Black Americans and even when they do not use a weapon to demand compliance they threaten police intervention as if the police work for them—and in some cases it feels like they do.

White citizens call 911 on Black citizens for the most mundane things—shopping, using a coupon, using a public park for family gatherings, renting vacation properties, swimming, taking out the trash, eating at a Subway, mowing the lawn, campaigning for votes, waiting for friends at a Starbucks—the list goes on and every month there seems to be a new video demonstrating that White citizens believe it their job to police Black Americans in the absence of real police presence. For example,

> A Starbucks employee called police on Dontre Hamilton who was sleeping in Milwaukee, Wisconsin's popular Red Arrow Park. Unbeknownst to Hamilton, the officer who shot him and the Starbucks employee, two officers had responded to an earlier call to check on the sleeping Hamilton and determined that he was not doing anything illegal. Therefore, they did not wake him. The Starbucks employee's call precipitated Hamilton's interaction with officer Christopher Manney. Manney arrived to the park and conducted an illegal stop and frisk while Dontre Hamilton was sleeping, which resulted in the two struggling over the officer's baton. Manney shot Dontre Hamilton fourteen times. It was later discovered that Hamilton suffered from schizophrenia and Hamilton's family believed he was confused and possibly feared that he was being attacked when the officer began to frisk him while still sleeping. Manney was fired from the police department for the illegal stop and frisk, but he was not charged in Hamilton's death. Hamilton's family sued and was awarded 2.3 million dollars from the City of Milwaukee. Hamilton's death is a prime example of citizens calling the police on black people and the dangerous and sometimes fatal repercussions that happen.[20]

In so many of these encounters captured on video, the White person asks for identification or asks what are you doing here—indicating that there has been a violation of White space. When White citizens call the police the Black person is usually chastised by police to appease the White caller, and when officers realize the silliness of the call they do not apologize. Another dynamic to the "I will call the police on you" threat is that when the Black person questions the real police why they are being questioned or detained at all, the officer threatens arrest. I should note that the offending White citizen is rarely chastised for their misuse of 911. What this says in the narrative of police/White citizen police interaction is that no matter what, Black

Americans do not have the right to question authority even though they are the ones who have been abused—sometimes physically and mentally from these interactions.

To understand the effects racism and microaggressions have on Black Americans' mental health, providers began researching the unconscious attitudes that White people held towards Black people. Researcher Joel Koval identified two forms of racism in America: dominative and aversive. Dominative racism is overt bigotry that is expressed openly and is mostly associated with hate groups like the Ku Klux Klan. Aversive racism is "subtle and indirect."[21] Dovidio and Gaertner hypothesize that "aversive racist sympathize with victims of past injustices, support the principle of racial equality, and regard themselves as non-prejudiced, but, at the same time possess negative feelings and beliefs about Blacks, which may be unconscious."[22]

Aversive racism is the foundation for what Dr. Chester M. Pierce describes as racial microaggressions, which are subtle conscious and unconscious racial interactions that contribute to diminished value of Black Americans. He urged researchers to look past the overt in your face racism and pay closer attention to the "subtle, cumulative miniassaults" that reproduce racism in environments like education and mass communication media.[23] These microaggressions can range from "racial slights, recurrent indignities and irritations, unfair treatment, stigmatization, hyper surveillance, and contentious personal attacks on one's wellbeing."[24] Smith, Yosso, and Solozaro expand Pierce's definition to include "layered insults based on one's race, race-gender, class, sexuality, language, immigration status, phenotype, access, or surname and cumulative insults that cause unnecessary stress to Black Americans."[25] The microaggressions captured in viral videos suggest that no matter how much money or education Blacks accumulate they will always be subjected to indignities because of the presumed superiority of Whites based on social categorization.[26]

White America's myth of superiority is rooted in the social categorization of two Americas—one White and one Black. Dovidio and Gaertner claim that social categorization plays a role in how people make meaning of their place in the world and the development of racial microaggressions. A group's placement in the hierarchy of social categorization is connected to the narrative circulated about the group in the national discourse. I call them narratives of mythological delusion because they are fixed stories that do not change no matter the amount of conflicting evidence to prove otherwise. The narratives of mythological delusion describe White Americans as heroic, inventive, and hardworking and describe Black Americans as cowardly, uneducated, and lazy.[27] James Baldwin in his essay "A Talk to Teachers" suggests, "It is the American White man who has long since lost his grip on reality. In some peculiar way, having created this myth about Negroes, and the myth about his own history, he created myths about the world" that prevent him from understanding the pent up frustrations of Black minorities.[28] These myths also suggest that Black people are culpable for the circumstances in their communities when "decades of solid and significant research on the larger structural forces that have plagued black urban communities"[29] emphatically proves otherwise. Baldwin suggests, as does Pierce, that American identity has a delusional component that propagates the illness of racism.

Pierce defined racism as a mental health illness with the potential to become an infectious disease for Black minorities and I highlight racial microaggressions because they affect the mental health of Black parents and their children and if reproductive activists are to help Black parents, we need to understand how these microaggressions are central to White privilege, over policing, and the mental health of Black citizens. The worry of will you be treated poorly, the worry of letting your young adults leave the house without you, the worry that your children will be racially profiled by police, the worry that White citizens will racially profile your children and worse treat them as adults and not children, the worry that you or your family members will not make it home after a police interaction all weight heavily on the psyche of Black families. When a mother insists her Black teenage son carry a neon pink phone case so his phone is not mistaken for a gun then you know the stakes are high for Black parents. The stress of racial microaggressions supports systemic racism and the mental health crisis that Black communities endure when parenting in the face of White citizen policing and for me these conversations have important consequences for the broader discussion of over policing of Black bodies, police interactions, racial profiling and the use of excessive force in our communities.

RESISTING RACIAL PROFILING AND POLICE VIOLENCE

The national outrage over the murders of unarmed Black citizens is popular because so many cell phone videos and audio exist of these dangerous interactions, but Black Americans have always known that we die at the hands of police because of racial profiling. Despite this body of visual evidence Black communities are still subjected to racial profiling, questionable arrests and prosecutions, and death by excessive force. The ACLU defines racial profiling as the targeting of "people of color for humiliating and often frightening detentions, interrogations, and searches without evidence of criminal activity and based on perceived race, ethnicity, national origin, or religion."[30] In 2019 *The Washington Post's Fatal Force* Database which tracks all police shootings resulting in a death, reports the following statistics,

2019	1,013
2018	992
2017	986
2016	962
2015	994[31]

Although it seems that police kill around the same number of people—I do wonder how many of these were truly justified. What this data says to me is that we have an ongoing problem with police interaction in communities of color.

Excessive force is an ongoing problem and Black mothers have taken it upon themselves to fight for change in their communities as a way to honor their dead children. They have found and are using their political voice to highlight the inequities that exist. The nation was paralyzed by the 2012 murder of Trayvon Martin at the hands of a *citizen cop*. We watched as Eric Garner was choked to death in July of 2014 and murdered by a gang of NYC police officers. Again, we watched Mike Brown walk with his hands up as he was shot by Saint Louis, MO, officer Darren Wilson in August of 2014. Again, in November of 2014 we watched as 12-year-old Tamir Rice was shot by Cleveland officer Timothy Loehmann. Again, we watched dashcam footage of Sandra Bland being arrested in July of 2015. She was later found dead in her cell. Again, we watched video of Philando Castille being shot by Jeronimo Yanez, a Minnesota officer in July of 2016. Again, we watched and heard bodycam video of Botham Jean's September 2018 murder by off duty officer Amy Guyger. Again, we listened to the audio of police bodycam video of Atatiana Jefferson being shot by officer Aaron Dean in October of 2019. Again, in February 2020 we watched video of Ahmaud Arbery being shot by two White citizen cops. These are the popular cases that made national news, but what of the stories that do not make national news? These tragedies represent loss of life, broken families left to mourn and make sense of what happened to their loved ones, trending social medial hashtags and a police force that automatically views Black bodies as a threat that must be dealt with forcefully.

Black mothers who have lost children to gun violence are engaging in the work of reproductive justice because when our children can leave home and roam freely in society and we expect they will return home, then reproductive activists have created a safe and healthy environment which is a core value of reproductive justice. Their fight is illustrative of the intersections of race, class and mothering. I suggest this because White women who are engaged in the fight against gun violence often focus on eradicating access to assault rifles used by mass shooters and changing gun laws, which is important, but very different from Black mothers' activism regarding this topic. For Black mothers, it is the removal of assault rifles and other weapons from the streets of their neighborhoods, reforming a justice system that removes civil liberties of the Black women, men, and children who are locked away, as well as protecting their families from dangerous cops who see excessive force as the standard for interacting with Black citizens—in all things we resist.

NOTES

1. Audre Lorde, "Man Child: A Black Lesbian Feminist's Response," in *Maternal Theory Essential Readings* ed. Andrea O'Reilly (Ontario: Demeter Press, 2007), chap. 9, Kindle.
2. bell hooks, "Homeplace A Site of Resistance" in *Maternal Theory Essential Readings* ed. Andrea O'Reilly (Ontario: Demeter Press, 2007), chap. 17, Kindle.
3. Loretta Ross and Rickie Solinger, *Reproductive Justice. An Introduction* (Oakland: University of California Press, 2017), 171.
4. Sandra Trappen, "What is the School-to-Prison Pipeline?" accessed December 21, 2019, https://sandratrappen.com/2018/08/27/school-resource-officers-the-school-to-prison-pipeline/.
5. American Civil Liberties Union (ACLU), "School-to-Prison Pipeline," accessed May 10, 2020, https://www.aclu.org/issues/juvenile-justice/school-prison-pipeline/school-prison-pipeline.
6. Defendants under the age of 18.
7. Wendy Sawyer, *Youth Confinement: The Whole Pie 2019*, Prison Policy Initiative. December 19, 2019. https://www.prisonpolicy.org/reports/youth2019.html. Accessed May 10, 2020.
8. Sawyer, *Youth Confinement*.
9. Artika Tyner, "The Emergence of the School-to-Prison Pipeline," *American Bar*, June 1, 2017. https://www.americanbar.org/groups/gpsolo/publications/gpsolo_ereport/2014/june_2014/the_emergence_of_the_school-to-prison_pipeline/, accessed December 21, 2019.
10. Anya Kamenetz, "Suspensions Are Down in U.S. Schools but Large Racial Gaps Remain," *NPR*, December 17, 2018. https://www.npr.org/2018/12/17/677508707/suspensions-are-down-in-u-s-schools-but-large-racial-gaps-remain.
11. Sandra Trappen, "What is the School-to-Prison Pipeline?" accessed May 10, 2020, https://sandratrappen.com/2018/08/27/school-resource-officers-the-school-to-prison-pipeline/.
12. Candice Petty, "School to Prison Pipeline," accessed May 10, 2020, https://2020club.org/school-to-prison-pipeline/. 2018.
13. Harold L. Rush, "Incarceration vs. Education in the United States of America Infographic," April 15, 2018, http://worktogether4peace.org/incarceration-vs-education-in-the-united-states-of-american-info-forward-by-harold-lee-rush/, accessed December 21, 2019.
14. Michelle Alexander, *The New Jim Crow: Mass Incarceration in the Age of Colorblindness* (New York: The New Press, 2012), 13.
15. Ruha Benjamin, *Race After Technology: Abolitionist Tools for the New Jim Code* (Cambridge: Polity Books, 2019).
16. Kimberly Harper, "Book Review of *Race After Technology: Abolitionist Tools for the New Jim Code*, Programmatic Perspectives."
17. I define White citizen police as White people who do not work for law enforcement but take on the role of surveilling when Black people enter into perceived *White spaces*.
18. Charles M. Pierce, "Psychiatric Problems of the Black Minority." In *American Handbook of Psychiatry*, ed. S. Arieti, 512–523 (New York: Basic Books, 1974), 512–523, 515.
19. Pierce, "Psychiatric Problems of the Black Minority," 515.

20. Kimberly Harper, "In the Fight of their Lives: Mothers of the Movement and the Pursuit of Reproductive Justice," *Reflections* 20, no. 2 (forthcoming fall 2020).
21. John F. Dovido and Samuel L. Gaertner, "Aversive Racism," *Advances in Experimental Social Psychology* 36 (2004): 1–52, 3.
22. Dovido and Samuel L. Gaertner, 3.
23. Pierce, "Psychiatric Problems of the Black Minority," 512–523, 515.
24. William A. Smith, Walter Allen, and Lynette L. Danley, "'Assume the Position . . . You Fit the Description': Psychological Experiences and Racial Battle Fatigue Among African American Male College Students," *American Behavioral Scientist* 51, no. 4 (December 1, 2007): 551–578.
25. William A. Smith, Man Hung, and Jeremy D. Franklin, "Racial Battle Fatigue and the MisEducation of Black Men: Racial Microaggressions, Societal Problems, & Environmental Stress," *The Journal of Negro Education* 80, no. 1 (December 21 2011): 63–82, 67.
26. Smith, Hung, and Franklin, "Racial Battle Fatigue," 67.
27. James Baldwin, "A Talk to Teachers," *The Saturday Review* (December 21, 1963): 42–44.
28. Baldwin, "A Talk."
29. Tricia Rose, *Hip Hop Wars: What We Talk About When We Talk About Hip Hop—and Why it Matters*, (New York: Basic Books, 2008), 9.
30. American Civil Liberties Union (ACLU), "Racial Profiling," accessed December 21, 2019. https://www.aclu.org/issues/racial-justice/race-and-criminal-justice/racial-profiling.
31. The Washington Post, *Fatal Force*, accessed December 19, 2019; May 10, 2020, https://www.washingtonpost.com/graphics/investigations/police-shootings-database/.

Conclusions

What I am suggesting with this entire body of work is that the institution of motherhood and the ethos of Black and White mothers are controlled by America's racist, patriarchal, and capitalistic ideologies. So what are we to do? Creating a more diverse healthcare workforce can help alleviate some of the implicit biases Black mothers face, but that is a long-term fix to a problem that has immediate consequences. After reading, writing, and talking about Black maternal health for the last eight years, it is clear that we have a lot of work to do and thankfully national attention is being placed on the maternal health crisis. While I am writing this final chapter, we are in the midst of a global pandemic, COVID-19, and people have been living under shelter in place laws passed by local and state governments for a little over a month. Neither my children nor I have seen friends or family. Shopping is limited and in order to do so, people are encouraged to wear a mask and gloves if possible, and in the midst of deaths around the nation and world women are still having babies. Due to the severity of the COVID-19 pregnant women are being limited in regard to the number of people they can have accompany them in the delivery room. So there's a new concern and urgency that Black mothers will once again find themselves alone, without an advocate or family members to serve as a support and witness to the actions of medical staff.

Amongst the confusion of COVID-19 and this work I consider where we are going and the research problems that follow from this. As an educator I ask myself what are the teaching tasks and what should our students be prepared to go out and do? I have two suggestions for future actions. We need a reimaging of what maternal health support looks like and we need implicit bias training for students and professionals in medicine, technical and professional communication, and computer science.

IMPLICIT BIAS AND RHETORICAL TRAINING IN ETHOS FOR MEDICAL PROFESSIONALS

The high maternal mortality rate and the anecdotal experiences of Black women are indications that medical professionals need training to recognize their own implicit biases so that all mothers can live to raise their children. As I have stated in the introduction and here again, Dr. Joia Crear-Perry is advocating that we move the discussion away from race as a risk factor and begin to talk about systemic racism and implicit bias as the real risk factors. So how do we do that? On a large scale this would require society to make changes at every level, and since I know this is not possible because America is just as committed to White supremacy as it is to democracy and freedom, my suggestion is to start with those who are on the frontlines of maternal health and that's our physicians, nurses, anesthesiologists, and related medical professionals. I would argue that most medical professionals did not and currently do not take any kind of course on implicit bias and if they do it is not reiterated in the workplace environment. So, a good solution would be to make implicit bias and a course on rhetorical ethos part of medical school curriculum. Topics likes these would also benefit from the support of professional organizations like the American Medical Association (AMA), American College of Obstetricians and Gynecologists (ACOG), and the American Association of Obstetricians and Gynecologists Foundation (AAOGF). Having a designation similar to the FACOG designation legitimizes the course and makes it an integral part of these organizations. If medical staff can see how stereotypes can unconsciously affect their opinion of Black mothers, they may be able to reconsider the decisions they make when providing care.

In addition to training for medical staff, I believe technical and professional communication (TPC) and computer science students need the same training. Collectively their work has the potential to influence much of what we see in public writing and in the digital world. TPC professionals write a variety of documents that support our institutions of learning, business, medicine, and beyond. Computer scientists create programs, algorithms, bots, software, and apps that shape our world online, so these professions matter a great deal. Imagine the well trained TPC graduate working at a government agency. She is responsible for researching and writing an annual report for law makers on issues of access to breast cancer screening. Rather than putting an image of women from all backgrounds on the cover and scattered throughout and then saying, "There I've included diversity in my research," she might consider how breast cancer affects each of these women differently along the lines of race, class, sexual orientation, gender, and access. The computer science graduate who has been asked to develop a webpage and app for cell phones might say, "Ok. I'm talking about breast cancer and I need to ensure that not only the images I select for the web page are diverse, but if I want women to interact using the app by creating their own avatar, I need to have a variety of ethnic skin tones and hair types represented." If either of these students have been trained through a social justice and reproductive justice lens, they might consider the intersecting identity of women as they research, create, and design. Representation matters and that's what students need to learn, analyze, and understand.

A REIMAGINING OF MATERNAL HEALTH

There needs to be a return to or a (re)imagining if you will of how mothers and their support systems view pregnancy. There needs to be a greater emphasis on maternal care for the sake of the mother and not the sake of the child. I know this sounds egregious, but society puts too much emphasis on the wellbeing of the child that we forget there is a mother. Thanks to the work of activists across the country, this is starting to take place. Congresswoman Dr. Alma Adams, Lauren Underwood and Senator Kamala Harris sponsored the Black Maternal Health Momnibus to help change health outcomes for Black mothers and all mothers. Momnibus is comprised of nine bills meant to do the following:

1. Make critical investments in social determinants of health that influence maternal health outcomes, like housing, transportation, and nutrition.
2. Provide funding to community-based organizations that are working to improve maternal health outcomes for Black women.
3. Comprehensively study the unique maternal health risks facing women veterans and invest in VA maternity care coordination.
4. Grow and diversify the perinatal workforce to ensure that every mom in America receives maternity care and support from people she can trust.
5. Improve data collection processes and quality measures to better understand the causes of the maternal health crisis in the United States and inform solutions to address it.
6. Invest in maternal mental health care and substance use disorder treatments.
7. Improve maternal health care and support for incarcerated women.
8. Invest in digital tools like telehealth to improve maternal health outcomes in underserved areas.
9. Promote innovative payment models to incentivize high-quality maternity care and continuity of health insurance coverage from pregnancy through labor and delivery and up to 1 year postpartum.[1]

As of today, May 10, 2020, the Bill has been introduced and referred to the subcommittee for Indigenous Peoples of the United States. In addition to the Momnibus, the Helping Moms Act of 2019 was introduced on November 18, 2019, and is an example of lawmakers attempting to support mothers. This act would extend postpartum from 60 days to one full year and it would be covered by Medicaid and the Children's Health Insurance Program (CHIP). According to Congress.gov the bill has been introduced and is waiting to move through the House of Representatives, Senate, and Office of the President before it becomes a law.[2]

Bills like the ones listed above are a move in the right direction. It shows that those on Capitol Hill understand the severity of this crisis; however, we still need boots on the ground to attend to the needs of Black mothers right now and that's why grassroots community-based organizations are so important. They fill in the gaps left by government agencies and are integral to the reproductive health of women.

Because Black mothers have a unique place in the landscape of America, our mothering is different. Our needs are different and our fight for reproductive justice is different. As such we must carve out places that affirm our lives and the lives of our children. At every stage of life, Black people are in danger and the staggering data suggests that given the political climate we live in today—thanks to President Trump's thinly veiled racist agenda and language—I sometimes fear things will get worse before they get better. Reproductive justice is hard work. Choosing to live authentically as a Black mother and raise children in a racialized society is hard work and emotionally taxing. Despite these hardships—joy exists. I see it every day in the faces of my students who are carefree and enjoying self-discovery. I see if in the faces of my children who are still unbothered by racism, and I see it in the faces of other mothers who whisper, "Girl you got it." "This too shall pass." "Take care of yourself, so you can take care of dem babies." While the image of Black motherhood is slow to change and may never change, Black women have not let society's ill-conceived perception stop them from demanding that their voice be heard and that is what is most important. Our Voice. Our Need. Our Action. Our RESISTANCE.

NOTES

1. Black Maternal Health Caucus, "About the Black Maternal Health Momnibus Act of 2020," accessed May 10, 2019, https://Blackmaternalhealthcaucus-underwood.house.gov/Momnibus.
2. Congress.Gov, Helping MOMS Act of 2019. accessed May 10, 2019, https://www.congress.gov/bill/116th-congress/house-bill/4996/actions?KWICView=false.

Appendix A

Level of Care Questionnaire

Q40: Do you believe African-American mothers receive the same level of maternal medical care as White mothers when dealing with labor and delivery staff. If yes, why?

#	Answer	%	Count
1	Yes	22	44
2	No	78	156
	Total	100	200

Q41: If yes, please explain why.

Because the color of our skin.

It's the professional and ethnical thing to do.

I think good medical care depends on the hospital. I chose a medical team that worked at good, reputable hospitals for maternity care which was also covered my insurance.

I was in a different area where care was better than other areas.

There was no other option to select, but in my case, I had an excellent staff. I had a condition that developed after 26 weeks gestation, and my prenatal providers were very attentive and took the necessary steps in order to deliver my baby safely. I cannot speak on others' experiences.

From my experience and from what I've heard through my White counterparts the level of care was the same. I don't feel like I missed out on any care that they've mentioned or I've heard about because I received all the same. But I'm coming from the standpoint of a married African American woman whose husband was present and at the hospital from start to finish. I don't believe that I've heard the same level of care was given to "single" African American women who may or may not have had the father of their child present.

I can only speak from my experience. I had a good relationship prior to getting pregnant.

I would know for sure.

I will hope that the medical staff see a pregnant woman and not the color of her skin.

I just did plenty of explaining.

At least for my first and second children, it appeared normal like the others around me.

I feel that I was treated with the same respect as a White mother:.

My labor and delivery went just as well as any other woman.

N/A

There was a mixture of ethnicity in the delivery room. Black nurses encouraged me as well as White ones.

From my experience, I was well cared for by the hospital staff.

No comment.

They came in the room a lot. Checked on me periodically.

I can only speak for my experience which was amazing all around so really can't compare it.

I didn't have a bad experience with my office or hospital to compare differently.

I can't speak for everyone else but my medical staff was attentive to my needs and made sure that everything went the way that I wanted it to, while also making sure they needed to do to make sure both me and my child were safe.

I really believe it all depends on your labor and delivery team. I received amazing care with both of my boys and both of my OBGYNs were White.

I did not feel as far as I could see that I or any other African American women in my presence were treated differently from White women or any other race.

N/A

I believe where my doctor resided, there was never a question that someone White receive better treatment then I.

I wouldn't know if they didn't.

I've witnessed it.

My staff was multiracial. They weren't biased at all.

I do not have facts to prove that we do not, my prenatal care and labor were positive experiences each time.

I believe that I did, I have no comparison. I was treated well, I do believe it was because I did have private medical insurance.

In my experience, on the labor and delivery unit everyone gets the same amount of attention relative to their demand. I don't think it's the same as the prenatal course.

I don't have anything to base it off of.

N/A

My pregnancy became high-risk and I delivered my child early - she was a preemie. I was admitted to the hospital and received the care I needed so I wouldn't deliver early.

I chose yes because there wasn't an option for not sure or I don't know. I haven't been exposed to that to make a comparison. I can say I seen the comparison between a Black mother and a African American doctor and a Caucasian doctor, the experience was not much different to what I encountered. The main focus was the wellbeing of the mother and the baby.

Have witnessed care provided.

I believe ethnicity plays a small part in any disparity in medical care for women. However, I think economics make a big difference.

N/A

Although my experience was a good one, I do believe African-American women who may not have certain levels of education and/or who are from lower socioeconomic backgrounds may be treated differently by medical experts.

Simply because I didn't not have a bad experience. I haven't spoken with any African American mothers who had bad experiences, but I would speculate that the issues are there.

It was my experience, although I know others feel differently.

I am not sure. Never asked anyone else about their experience.

I feel both pregnancies I had support for my overall welfare of the babies. I think if they see you and partner are serious then they will respond accordingly.

I can only base my answer on my experience. I had a great medical team and a good birth experience.

I had great insurance.

One with insurance maybe, but those on Medicaid probably not.

I have not experienced/seen a difference.

In my experience, the staff appeared to show all patients the same care and respect. I did not notice any special treatment or lack of care or professionalism.

Appendix B

Emergency C-Section Stories.

Q75: Please share the circumstances that required you to need an emergency C-section.

Fluid on baby B (twins) was low. waited a week to see if it would normalize. it never did as it kept leaking to where he barely had amniotic fluid.

Dips in the heart rate.

Umbilical cord wrapped around babies neck.

The baby's heart rate dropped.

The baby was in danger or was not getting enough oxygen.

Once induced baby still would start birthing in time so doctor wanted to do C-section.

My son was growth restricted and his heart rate would drop during the induced contractions.

My daughters cord was wrapped around her neck.

My daughter heart rate kept dropping.

My amino fluid was low, but I wasn't having contractions, so they tried to induce labor. I never dilated and my son would be in distress with every contraction. So we had a C-section.

My BP dropped.

Meconium.

Labor was not progressing and the baby was becoming stressed.

In labor for 54 hours. Fear of infection or dry birth.

I went in for a checkup and blood pressure was high and it also seemed that my doctor would be off that weekend. I was induced on a Thursday and my child did not arrive until Saturday.

I was induced because a week after my due date, my child still didn't want to come. I stopped dilating at 3 cm. After 32 hours, I got a fever and he had pooped on himself (meconium?). So they did a C-section.

I was 7 days beyond my due date. The medication given to induce my labor was not working.

I had been in labor for 12 hours and had not dilated as quickly as the doctor wanted me to. I was working with a midwife, through my healthcare provider, but her shift had just completed. So when she left within 30 minutes of shift change the White male doctor (whom I hadn't seen prior to this) came in to announce I'd be having a C-section. I didn't have any say in it and looking back would have made other requests if I had had information prior to that moment. (Hindsight is 20/20.)

I had a routine appointment earlier that day and everything was fine. After I left, I felt my son was not moving as much as he normally did and went to the hospital. They said my "bag of waters" was low and that he was bumping against his chord.

Hypertension.

Heart rate dropped.

For First Child, I was induced, in labor for 22 hours, with no progress, Baby was in posterior position.

Due to baby heart rate dropping because of the medication given to induce.

Cord wrapped around his neck.

Child's heart beat racing and stressing her out.

Both my baby and I were in distress after almost two days of labor. I was a week overdue but my water never broke, I never fully dilated.

Baby's heart rate was in the 200's sustained. I also had fever and vomiting.

Baby wasn't coming out and in distress.

Baby heart stopped beating. Second time our vitals were dropping.

Baby heart rate was elevated, mommy blood pressure was elevated.

"Failure to Progress." Doctors stated that I was not dilating quick enough.

Bibliography

Adams, Alma. "Congresswomen Adams and Underwood Launch Black Maternal Health Caucus." Congresswoman Alma Adams, April 19, 2019. https://adams.house.gov/media-center/press-releases/congresswomen-adams-and-underwood-launch-black-maternal-health-caucus.
Akbar, Na'im. *Know Thy Self.* Talllahassee: Mind Production and Associates, 1998.
Alexander, Michelle. *The New Jim Crow: Mass Incarceration in the Age of Colorblindness.* New York: The New Press, 2012.
American Civil Liberties Union. "Racial Profiling." https://www.aclu.org/issues/racial-justice/race-and-criminal-justice/racial-profiling. Accessed December 21, 2019.
American Civil Liberties Union. "School to Prison Pipeline." https://www.aclu.org/issues/juvenile-justice/school-prison-pipeline/school-prison-pipeline. Accessed May 10, 2020.
The American College of Obstetricians and Gynecologists. "Ectopic Pregnancy, Frequently Asked Questions" (Washington: American College of Obstetricians and Gynecologists). Accessed November 29, 2019.
Anderson, Carol. *White Rage: The Unspoken Truth of Our Racial Divide.* New York: Bloomsbury Publishing, 2017.
Associated Press. "Lawmaker Says He Didn't Research Ectopic Pregnancy Procedure Before Adding to Bill," WOSU Public Media, December 12, 2019. https://radio.wosu.org/post/lawmaker-says-he-didnt-research-ectopic-pregnancy-procedure-adding-bill#stream/0.
Bahr, Anna. 2012. "As Memoires of Dalkon Shield Fade, Women Embrace IUDs Again." *Ms. Magazine*, August 29, 2012. https://msmagazine.com/2012/08/29/as-memories-of-dalkon-shield-fade-women-embrace-iuds-again/.
Baldwin, James. "A Talk to Teachers." *The Saturday Review* (December 21, 1963): 42–44.
Ball, Elaine. *Not Our Kind of Girl. Unraveling the Myths of Black Teenage Motherhood.* Berkeley: Univeristy of California Press, 1997.
Barton, Ben F. and Martha Lee Barton. "Ideology and the Map: Toward a Postmodern Visual Design Pratice." In *Central Works in Technical Communication*, edited by Johndan Johnson-Eilola and Stuart Selber, 232–251. New York: Oxford Univerty Press, 2004.
Baumlin, James and Craig Meyer. "Positioning Ethos in/for the Twenty-First Century: An Introduction to Histories of Ethos." *Humanities* 2018 7, 78.
Baumlin, James and Tita French Baumlin. *Ethos New Essays in Rhetorical and Critical Theory.* Dallas: Southern Methodist University Press, 1994.
Benjamin, Ruha. *Race After Technology.* Cambridge: Policy Books, 2019.
Bezusko, Adriane."Criminalizing Black Motherhood." *Souls* 15: 1–2: 39–55. 2013.
Black Maternal Health Caucus, "About the Black Maternal Health Momnibus Act of 2020."

Bibliography

Bliss, Kevin. "Lawsuit: Woman Gave Birth Alone in Colorado Jail Cell," *Prison Legal News*, October 7, 2019. https://www.prisonlegalnews.org/news/2019/oct/7/lawsuit-woman-gave-birth-alone-colorado-jail-cell/.

Britton, Earl. "What Is Technical Writing?" *College Composition and Communication* 16, no. 2 (1965): 113–116.

Buchanan, Lindal. *Rhetorics of Motherhood*. Carbondale: Southern Illinois University, 2013.

Center for Reproductive Rights. *Research Overview of Maternal Mortality and Morbidity in the United States*. New York: Center for Reproductive Rights, 2016.

Christie, Chris."The President's Commission on Combating Drug Addiction and the Opioid Crisis," *The Presidents Commission*, 2017. https://www.whitehouse.gov/sites/whitehouse.gov/files/images/Final_Report_Draft_11-1-2017.pdf.

Cohen, Susan, A. "Abortion and Women of Color: The Bigger Picture." *The Guttmacher Policy Review* (New York: The Guttmacher Institute, August 6, 2008), 2. https://www.guttmacher.org/gpr/2008/08/abortion-and-women-color-bigger-picture.

Collins, Craig. "Toxic Racism. The Struggle for Environmental Justice. My neighborhood is Killing Me." In *Slide Share*, June 16, 2014. https://www.slideshare.net/CraigCollins2/toxic-racism-the-struggle-for-environmental-justice.

Collins, Patrica. *Black Feminist Thought: Knowledge Consciousness, and the Politics of Empowerment*. New York: Routledge, 1991.

———. *Black Sexual Politics: African American, Gender, and the New Racism*. New York: Routledge, 2004.

———. "The Meaning of Motherhood in Black Culture and Mother-Daughter Relationships" in *Maternal Theory Essential Readings* edited by Andrea O'Reilly, 274–289, Ontario: Demeter Press, 2007.

Congress.Gov. "Helping MOMS Act of 2019." https://www.congress.gov/bill/116th-congress/house-bill/4996/actions?KWICView=false. Accessed May 10, 2019.

Crear-Perry, Joia. "Race Isn't a Risk Factor in Maternal Health. Racism Is." *Rewire News*, April 11, 2018, https://rewire.news/article/2018/04/11/maternal-health-replace-race-with-racism/.

Cullors, Patrice. "#Justice4Kyira Means Justice for Black Mothers Everywhere." *The Root*, June 22, 2017. https://www.theroot.com/justice4kyira-means-justice-for-black-mothers-everywhe-1796340568. Accessed June 18, 2017.

David, Marlo. "State Violence and Pregnant Black Mothers." *African American Intellectual History Society*, July 24, 2018. https://www.aaihs.org/state-violence-and-pregnant-black-mothers.

DeLee, Joseph B. "The Prophylactic Forceps Operation." *American Journal of Obstetrics and Gynecology* 1, no. 34 (1920): 33–44.

Diangelo, Robin. 2018. *White Fragility: Why It's so Hard for White People to Talk about Racism*. Boston: Beacon Press, 2018.

Donawerth, Jane. *Rhetorical Theory by Women Before 1900: An Anthology*. Lanham: Rowman & Littlefield, 2002.

Dovido, John F and Samuel L. Gaertner, "Aversive Racism." *Advances in Experimental Social Psychology* 36 (2004): 1–52.

Dreher, Tanja. "Listening Across Differences: Media and Multiculturalism Beyond the Politics of Voice." *Journal of Media and Cultural Studies* 23, no. 4 (August 2009): 445–458.

Du Bois, W. E. B. "Black Folk and Birth Control," *Birth Control Review* 16, no. 6 (1932).

Eastern Illinois University, "Bulletin 220—The Lincoln-Douglas Debate at Charleston, IL September 18, 1858" (1957). Eastern Illinois University Bulletin. 60. http://thekeep.eiu.edu/eiu_bulletin/60.

Emmrich, Stuart. "President Trump Seems to Have a Problem with Yamiche Alcindor. I Wonder Why." *Vogue* (March 31, 2020). https://www.vogue.com/article/yamiche-alcindor-donald-trump-feud.

Epstein, Rebecca, Jamilia J. Blake, and Thalia Gonzales. "Girlhood Interrupted: The Erasure of Black Girls' Childhood." Washington, DC: Georgetown Law School Center on Poverty and Inequality, 2017.

Fairclough, Norman. *Analysing Discourse*. New York: Routledge, 2003.

Bibliography 121

———. *Critical Discourse Analysis: The Critical Study of Language.* London: Longman Group Limited, 1995.
———. *Language and Power.* London: Routledge, 2013.
FitzGerald, Chloe and Samia Hurst, "Implicit Bias in Healthcare Professionals: A Systematic Review" *BMC Medical Ethics* 18, no. 19 (March 1, 2017): 1–182. https://doi.org/10.1186/s12910-017-0179-8.
Flexner, Abraham. "*Medical Education in America. Rethinking the Training of American Doctors.*" *The Atlantic.* 1910. https://www.theatlantic.com/magazine/archive/1910/06/medical-education-in-america/306088/.
Fried, Marlene Gerber. "Reproductive Rights Activism after Roe." In *Radical Reproductive Justice*, edited by Loretta J. Ross, Lynn Roberts, Erika Derkas, Whitney Peoples, and Pamel Bridgwater Toure, 139–150. New York: Feminist Press, 2017.
Gammage, Marquita, M. *Representations of Black Women in the Media: The Damnation of Black Womanhood.* New York: Routledge, 2016.
Giddings, Paula. *When and Where I Enter.* New York: William Morrow, 1984.
Glenn, Cheryl. *Unspoken: A Rhetoric of Silence.* Carbondale: Southern Illinois University Press, 2004.
Glymph, Thavolia.*Out of the House of Bondage: The Transformation of the Plantation Household.* New York: Cambridge University Press, 2008.
Goode, Keisha L. "Birthing, Blackness, and the Body: Black Midwives and Experiential Continuities of Institutional Racism." PhD diss., City University of New York, 2014.
Guasco, Michael. "The Misguided Focus on 1619 as the Beginning of Slavery in the U.S. Damages Our Understanding of American History." *Smithsonian Magazine*, September 13, 2017. https://www.smithsonianmag.com/history/misguided-focus-1619-beginning-slavery-us-damages-our-understanding-american-history-180964873/.
Guttmacher Institute. "State Facts About Abortion: North Carolina." (New York: Guttmacher Institute, 2017), 2. https://www.guttmacher.org/sites/default/files/factsheet/sfaa-nc_2.pdf.
Hanna-Attisha, Mona, Jenny LaChance, Richard Casey Sadler, and Allison Champney Schnepp. "Elevated blood lead levels in children assicated with the Flint drinking water crisis: A spatial analysis of risk and public health response." *American Journal of Public Health* 106, no. 2 (January 16, 2016): 283–290.
Hall, William J., Mimi V. Chapman, Kent M. Lee, Yesenia M. Merion, Tainayah W. Thomas, B. Keith Payne, and Eugenia Eng, Steven H. Day, and Tamera Coyne-Beasley. "Implicit Racial/Ethnic Bias among Health Care Professionals and Its Influence on Health Care Outcomes: A Systematic Review." *American Journal of Public Health* 105, no.12 (2015): 60–76.
Harper, Kimberly. "Black Lives Don't Matter Because Black Wombs Don't Matter. Exploring the Repoductive Rights of Black Mothers." In *Writing Networks for Social Justice*, edited by Donald Unger and Liz Lane,52–55. 4C4equality, 2017.
———. "Implicit Bias, Visual Rhetoric, and Black Maternal Health: Understanding the Real Risk Factor." In *Band-Aids to Scalpels: Motherhood Experiences in/of Medicine*, edited by Rohini Bannerjee and Karim Mukhida. Ontario: Demeter Press, April 2021.
———. "In the Fight of Their Lives: Mothers of the Movement and the Pursuit of Reproductive Justice." *Reflections* 20, no. 2 (forthcoming fall 2020).
———. Book Review of Race After Technology: Abolitionist Tools for the New Jim Code Programmatic Perspectives.
Hatchett, Glenda. "Judge Hatchett in Her Own Legal Battle After Daughter-in-Law Dies Shortly After Giving Birth: Interview with Judge Hackett." By Jim Moret. May 16, 2017.
Herndl, Carl. "Teaching Discourse and Reproducing Culture." In *Central Work in Technical Communication*, edited by Johndan Johnson-Eilola and Stuart A. Selber, 222–231. Oxford Univeristy Press: New York, 2004.
History.com, "Roe v. Wade is Decided," *This Day in History* (History.com, November 13, 2009), https://www.history.com/topics/womens-rights/roe-v-wade.
Hoffman, Kelly, Sophie Trawalter, JordanR. Axt, and M. Normal Oliver. "Racial Bias in Pain Assessment and Treatment Recommendations, and False Beliefs about Biological Differ-

ences Between Blacks and Whites." *Proceedings of the National Academy of Sciences of the United States of America* (April 19, 2016): 4296–4301.

Holmes, David, G. *Revisiting Racialized Voice: African American Ethos in Language and Literature*. Carbondale: Southern Illinois University, 2004.

hooks, bell. *Ain't I a Woman, Black Women and Feminism*. Boston: South End Press, 1981.

———. *Talking Back Thinking Feminist, Thinking Black*. New York: Routledge, 2015.

———. "Homeplace A Site of Resistance" in *Maternal Theory Essential Readings* edited by Andrea O'Reilly, 266–273, Ontario: Demeter Press, 2007.

Hunter, Lynette. "Ideology as the Ethos of the Nation State." *Rhetorica: A Journal of the History of Rhetoric* 14, no. 2 (Spring 1996): 197–229.

Jefferson, Thomas, Benjamin Franklin, John Adams, Roger Sherman, and Rober R. Livingston. July 4, Copy of Declaration of Independence. July 4, 1776. Manuscript/Mixed Material. https://www.loc.gov/item/mtjbib000159/.

Jones, Natasha. "The Technical Communicator as Advocate: Integrating a Social Justice Approach in Technical Communication." *Journal of Technical Writing and Communication* 46, no. 3 (2016): 342–361, 345.

Jones, Rachel. "Why Giving Birth in the US is Surprisingly Deadly." January 2019. *National Geographic*. https://www.nationalgeographic.com/magazine/2019/01/giving-birth-in-united-states-suprisingly-deadly/.

Kamenetz, Anya. "Suspensions Are Down in U.S. Schools But Large Racial Gaps Remain," *NPR*, December 17, 2018. https://www.npr.org/2018/12/17/677508707/suspensions-are-down-in-u-s-schools-but-large-racial-gaps-remain.

Kaplan, Elaine Bell. *Not Our Kind of Girl: Unraveling the Myths of Black Teenage Motherhood*. Berkeley: University of California Press, 1997.

Kendi, Ibram X. *Stamped from the Beginning: The Definitive History of Racist Ideas in America*. New York: National Books, 2016.

Kenney, Keith. "Building Visual Communication Theory by Borrowing from Rhetoric," in *Visual Rhetoric in a Digital World* ed. Carolyn Handa." New York: Bedford St. Martin's, 2004, 332–343.

Koerber, Amy. *Breast or Bottle: Contemporary Controversies in Infant-Feeding Policy and Practices*. Columbia: Univeristy of South Carolina Press, 2013.

Kruse, Karen. "Simkins v. Cone." *Encyclopedia of North Carolina*. Chapel Hill: Univeristy of Chapel Hill, 2006. https://www.ncpedia.org/simkins-v-cone.

Lakoff, George and Mark Johnson. *Metaphors We Live By*. Chicago: University of Chicago Press, 1980.

Lawson, Erica. "Black Women's Mothering in a Historical Contemporary Perspective: Understanding the Past, Forgiving the Future." *Journal of Association for Research on Mothering* (2000): 21–30.

Lay, Mary. *The Rhetoric of Midwifery. Gender, Knowledge, and Power*. New Brunswick: Rutgers Univeristy Press, 2000.

Little, Becky. "How a Movement to Send Freed Slaves to Africa Created Liberia." www.history.com. April 5, 2010. https://www.history.com/news/slavery-american-colonization-society-liberia. https://www.legislature.ohio.gov/legislation/legislation-documents?id=GA133-HB-413. Accessed. November 29, 2019.

Logan, Enid. "The Wrong Race. Committing Crime, Doing Drugs, and Maladjusted for Motherhood: The Nation's Fury Over "Crack Babies." *Social Justice* 26, no. 1 (1999): 115–138.

Logan, Shirley Wilson. *With Pen and Voice. A Critical Anthology of Nineteenth-Century African-American Women*. Carbondale: Southern Illinois University Press, 1995.

Lorde, Audre. "The Transformation of Silence into Language and Action." Paper delivered at the Modern Language Association's Lesbian and Literature Panel, Chicago, Illinois, December 28, 1977.

———. "Man Child: A Black Lesbian Feminist's Response" in *Maternal Theory Essential Readings* edited by Andrea O'Reilly, Ontario: Demeter Press, 2007, chap. 9, Kindle.

Leavitt, Judith Walzer. "Joseph B. DeLee and the Practice of Preventive Obstetrics." *American Journal of Public Health* 78, no. 10 (October 1998): 1353–1360.

Luke, Jenny M. *Delivered by Midwives: African American Midwifery in the Twentieth-Century South*. Jackson: University Press of Mississippi, 2018.
Madgett, Katherine. "Sheppard-Towner Maternity and Infancy Protection Act (1921)." *The Embryo Project Encyclopedia*. May 18, 2017. http://embryo.asu.edu/handle/10776/11503.
Martin, Jonathan. "Simkins v. Cone (1963)." North Carolina History Project. May 8, 2020. https://northcarolinahistory.org/encyclopedia/simkins-v-cone-1963/.
Martin, Nina, and Renee Montagne. "Black Mothers Keep Dying after Giving Birth, Shalon Irving's Story Explains Why." *All Things Considered*, National Public Radio. December 7, 2017. 12 minutes. https://www.npr.org/2017/12/07/568948782/black-mothers-keep-dying-after-giving-birth-shalon-irvings-story-explains-why.
McDaniels, Dani. *We Live for the We. The Political Power of Black Motherhood*. New York: Bold type Books, 2019.
Mendez, Adrianna. "North Carolina Woman Pays Addicts to Get on Long-term Birth Control or Get Sterilized." Aired February 20, 2018 on News 13WLOS. https://wlos.com/news/local/north-carolina-woman-pays-addicts-for-long-birth-control-or-sterilization.
Mills, Sara. *Discourse*. 2nd ed. New York: Routledge, 2004.
Moore, Patrick. "Instrumental Discourse is as Humanistic as Rhetoric." *Journal of Business and Technical Communication* 10, no. 1 (1996): 100–118.
Morrison, Toni. *Playing in the Dark Whiteness and the Literary Imagination*. New York: First Vintage Books Edition, 1993.
———. "A Humanist View," Portland State University's Oregon Public Speakers Collection: "Black Studies Center Public Dialogue. Pt 2 (May 30, 1975).
———. "Toni Morrison Uncensored." Interviewed by Jana Wendt. Audio. 1998 https://www.youtube.com/watch?v=DQ0mMjII22I.
Moynihan, Patrick.*The Negro Family: The Case for National Action*. Office of Policy Planning and Research, United States Department of Labor, 1965.
Murphy, Carrie. "According to Pregnancy Books, Only White Women Get Pregnant." *Mommyish*, January 24, 2014. https://www.mommyish.com/women-of-color-childbirth/.
National Institutes of Health. "NIH HEAL Initiative Research Plan." US Department of Health and Human Services. Updated March 18, 2020. https://www.nih.gov/research-training/medical-research-initiatives/heal-initiative/heal-initiative-research-plan.
National Partnership for Women and Families. "Snapshot: Black Maternal Health in the United States." National Partnership for Women and Families. April 2018. https://www.nationalpartnership.org/our-work/resources/healthcare/maternity/maternity-snapshot-black-maternal-health.pdf.
Ocen, Pricilla A. "Punishing Pregnancy: Race, Incarceration, and the Shackling of Pregnant Prisoners." *California Law Review* 100, no. 5 (October 2012): 1239–1311.
O'Reilly, Andrea. *Maternal Theory: Essential Readings*. Ontario: Demeter Press, 2007.
Owens, Kim. *Writing Childbirth: Women's Rhetorical Agency in Labor and Online*. Carbondale: Southern Illinois University, 2015.
Pearson, Catherine. "Black Women Face More Trauma During Childbirth." *Huffington Post*, June 6, 2018. https://www.huffingtonpost.com/entry/black-women-childbirth-mortality-trauma_us_5b045eaae4b0784cd2af0f71.
Petty, Candice. "School to Prison Pipeline" https://2020club.org/school-to-prison-pipeline/. 2018. Access May 10, 2020.
Perkins, Linda. "The Impact of the "Cult of True Womanhood on the Education of Black Women." *Journal of Social Issues* 39, no. 3 (1983): 17–28.
Pierce, Charles, M. "Psychiatric Problems of the Black Minority." In *American Handbook of Psychiatry*, edited by S. Arieti, 512–523. New York: Basic Books.
Pincus, Jane. "Foreward." *The Rhetoric of Pregnancy*. Chicago: The University of Chicago Press, 2014.
Pinto-Correia, Clara. "Technological Motherhood." In *Fear, Wonder, and Science in the New Age of Reproductive Biotechnology*, edited by Scott Gilbert and Clara Pinto-Correia, 107–126. New York: Columbia University Press, 2017.
Pittman, Coretta. "Black Women Writers and the Trouble with Ethos: Harriet Jacobs, Billie Holiday, and Sister Souljah." *Rhetoric Society Quarterly* 37, no. 1 (Winter 2007): 43–70.

Ratcliff, Krista. *Rhetorical Listening Identification, Gender, Whiteness*. Carbondale: Southern Illinois University Press, 2005.
Reynolds, Nedra."Ethos as Location: New Sites for Understanding Discursive Authority," *Rhetoric Review* 11, no. 2 (Spring 1993): 325–338.
Roberts, Dorothy. *Killing the Black Body: Race Reproduction, and the Meaning of Liberty*. New York: Random House, 1997.
———. "Unshackling Black Motherhood." *The Michigan Law Review 95* (February 1997): 983–964, https://scholarship.law.upenn.edu/faculty_scholarship/1322.
Robinson, Zoe. "Constitutional Personhood." *The George Washington Law Review* 84, no. 3 (May 2016): 605–667.
Rose, Trica. *Hip Hop Wars: What we Talk About When We Talk About Hip-Hop—and Why it Matters*. New York: Basic Books, 2008.
Rosenthal, Lisa, and Marci Lobel. "Stereotypes of black american women related to sexuality and motherhood." *Pyschology of Women Quarterly* 40, no. 3 (2016): 414–427.
Rosner, David. "Flint, Michigan: A Century of Environmental Injustice." *American Journal of Public Health Editorials* 106, no. 2 (February 2016): 200–201.
Ross, Loretta J. "African-American Women and Abortion: A Neglected History." *Journal of Health Care for the Poor and Underserved* 3, no. 2 (1992): 274–284.
———. "Reproductive Justice as Intersectional Feminist Activism." *Souls* 19, no. 3 (2017): 286–314.
Ross, Loretta, Lynn Roberts, Erika Derkas, Whitney Peoples, and Pamlea Bridgewater Toure. *Radical Reproductive Justice*. New York: Feminist Press, 2017.
Ross, Loretta and Rickie Solinger. *Reproductive Justice. An Introduction*. Oakland: University of California Press, 2017.
Rothman, Barbara. *Recreating Motherhood*. New Brunswick: Rutgers Univeristy Press, 2000.
Rousseau, Nicole. "Social Rhetoric and the Construction of Black Motherhood." *Journal of Black Studies* (2013): 451–471.
Royster, Jacqueline Jones. "When the First Voice You Hear is Not Your Own," *College Composition and Communication* 47, no. 1 (February 1996): 29–40.
Rush, Harold L. "Incarceration vs. Education in the United States of America Infographic." Worktogether4peace, April 15, 2019. http://worktogether4peace.org/incarceration-vs-education-in-the-united-states-of-american-info-forward-by-harold-lee-rush/.
Sawyer, Wendy.*Youth Confinement: The Whole Pie 2019*. Prison Policy Initiative. December 19, 2019. https://www.prisonpolicy.org/reports/youth2019.html. Accessed May 10, 2020.
Schmertz, Johanna. "Constructing Essences: Ethos and the Postmodern Subject of Feminism." *Rhetoric Review* 18, no. 1 (Autumn, 1999): 82–91. https://www.jstor.org/stable/466091.
Schur, Richard. "Haunt or Home? Ethos and African American Literature." *Humanities* 7, no. 80 (2018): 4–13.
Schwartz, Marie J. *Birthing a Slave: Motherhood and Medicine in the Antebellum South*. Cambridge: Harvard University Press, 2009.
Seigel, Marika. *The Rhetoric of Pregnancy*. Chicago: University of Chicago Press, 2014.
Settles, Isis H., Jennifer S. Pratt-Hyatt, and Nicole T. Buchanan. "Through the Lens of Race: Black and White Women's Perceptions of Womanhood." *Psychol Woman Q.*, 2008.
Smith, William A., Allen Walter, and Lynette Danley. "Assume the Position . . . You Fit the Description." Psychological Experiences and Racial Battle Fatigue Among African American Male College Students." *American Behavioral Scientist* 51, no. 4 (December 2007): 551–578.
Smith, William A., Man Hung, and Jeremy D. Franklin. "Racial Battle Fatigue and the MisEducation of Black Men: Racial Microaggressions, Societal Problems, & Environmental Stress." *The Journal of Negro Education* 80, no.1 (December 21 2011): 63–82.
Smith, Philip W., Kristin Watkins, and Angel Hewlett. "Infection Control Through the Ages." *American Journal of Infection Control* 40 (2012): 35–42.
Solinger, Rickie. *Pregnanacy and Power: A Short History of Reproductive Politics in America*. New York: New York Univeristy Press, 2005.

Solinger, Rickie. "Race and "Value": Black and White Illegitimate Babies, 1945–1965." In *Mothering, Ideology, Experience, and Agency*, edited by Evelyn Nakano Glenn, Grace Chang, and Linda Rennie Forcey, 287–310. New York: Routledge, 1994.
Taney, Roger. "Opinion of the Court." Dred Scott v. Sandford, 60 U.S. 393 (1856), 405–407. Accessed December 12, 2019. https://www.law.cornell.edu/supremecourt/text/60/393.
Thiele, Rebecca. "Road Salt Contaminating Drinking Water." *Fresh Air Weekend*, Aired November 24, 2015, on WMUK 102.1. http://wmuk.org/post/road-salt-contaminating-drinking-water-urban-lakes.
Toure, Pamela Bridgewater. "Transforming Silence." In *Racial Reproductive Justice: Foundations, Theory, Practice, and Critique*, edited by Loretta J. Ross, Lynn Roberts, Erika Derkas, Whitney Peoples, and Pamela Bridgewater Toure, 233–237. New York: Feminist Press, 2017.
Trappen, Sandra. "What is the School-to-Prison Pipeline?" Dr. Sandra Trappen. August 27, 2018. https://sandratrappen.com/2018/08/27/school-resource-officers-the-school-to-prison-pipeline/.
Turner, Sasha. "The Nameless and the Forgotten: Maternal Grief, Sacred Protection, and the Archive of Slavery." *Slavery & Abolition*, 232–250: 2017. Need vol. and issue for this source.
Tyner, Artika. "The Emergence of the School-to-Prison Pipeline." American Bar Association, June 1, 2014. https://www.americanbar.org/groups/gpsolo/publications/gpsolo_ereport/2014/june_2014/the_emergence_of_the_school-to-prison_pipeline/.
van Dijk, Teun A. "Discourse and the Denial of Racism." In *The Discourse Reader*, edited by Adam Jaworski and Nikolas Coupland, 541–558. New York: Routledge, 1999.
Villarosa, Linda. "Why America's Black Mothers and Babies Are in a Life-or-Death Crisis." *New York Times*, April 11, 2018. https://www.nytimes.com/2018/04/11/magazine/black-mothers-babies-death-maternal-mortality.html.
The Washington Post. "Fatal Force Report." Accessed December 19, 2019 and May 10, 2020. https://www.washingtonpost.com/graphics/investigations/police-shootings-database/.
Washington, Harriet. *Medical Apartheid: The Dark History of Medical Experimentation: Black Americans from Colonial Times to the Present.* New York: First Anchor Books, 2006.
Webster, Crystal Lynn. "In Pursuit of Autonomous Womanhood: Nineteenth-Century Black Motherhood in the U.S. North." *Slavery & Abolition* 38, no. 2: 425–440. 2017.
Welter, Barbara. "The Cult of True Womanhood: 1820–1860." *American Quarterly* 18, no. 2 (1966): 151–174, https://www.legislature.ohio.gov/legislation/legislation-documents?id=GA133-HB-413.
Wiltshire, Jaqueline, Jeroan J. Allison, Roger Brown, and Keith Elder. "African American Women Perceptions of Physician Trustworthiness: A Factorial Survey Analysis of Physician Race, Gender, and Age." *AIMS Public Health* 5, no. 2 (May 17, 2018): 122–134.
Yetman, Norman. *When I was a Slave: Memoirs from the Slave Narrative Collection.* Mineola: Dover Publications, 2002.
Young, Allison. "U. S. Most Dangerous Place to Give Birth in Developed World, USA Today Investigation Finds." Interviewed by Gayle King, Nora O' Donnell and John Dickerson. CBC News, July 26, 2018. Podcast, 05: 21. https://www.cbsnews.com/news/us-most-dangerous-place-to-give-birth-in-developed-world-usa-today-investigation-finds/.

Index

abortion, 77–81
ACLU (American Civil Liberties Union), 98
acquired immunity transmission, 5–7, 28–29
ACS (American Colonization Society), 23
Adams, Alma, xv, 111
adoption system, 34
AFDC (Aid to Families with Dependent Children), 32, 39–41
A.H. Robin Company, 76
Aid to Families with Dependent Children (AFDC), 32, 39–41
Akbar, Na'im, 5
Alcindor, Yamiche, 59
Alexander, Michele, 100
Alfonso V of Portugal, King, 12
amazon.com search for pregnancy books, 66, 67. *See also* visual images of motherhood
American Civil Liberties Union (ACLU), 98
American Colonization Society (ACS), 23
American ideology, 50–52
anesthesia in medical experiments, 19
angry Black woman trope, 59
antebellum era: anti-Black sentiment during, 1–5; enslaved mothers, 5–7; freedwomen in the North, 8; gynecological complications during, 16–18; medical experimentation during,

18–19; midwifery and physicians, 86; value of Black women during, 29. *See also* breeder women; chattel slavery; mammy image
Arbery, Ahmaud, 102, 105
Aristotle, 52
authors as gatekeepers, 71
aversive racism, 103–104

bad Black mother trope, 33, 56, 57
Baldwin, James, 103
Barnes & Noble search for pregnancy books, 66, 68. *See also* visual images of motherhood
barren women, 14
Barton, Ben, 73
Barton, Martha Lee, 73
Baumlin, James S., 52
Baumlin, Tita French, 52
birth control. *See* contraception
Black bodies, xvi, 8, 11, 12, 14, 93
Black Maternal Caucus, xv
Black Maternal Health Momnibus, 111–112
Black men: castration of, 32; "man in the house rule," 32; protected through silence, 59; stereotypes of, 2–3, 12, 14
Black midwifery: challenges of, 91–92; granny midwives, 86, 87; historical perspective, 85–89; hospital access and, 89–90; medical doctors in competition

127

with, 85–88; nurse midwives, 92–95; racism and, 88; Sheppard-Towner Maternity and Infancy Act, 88–89; stigma of home births, 91–92. *See also* childbirth; maternal healthcare; pregnancy
Black Sexual Politics (Collins), 39
Black stereotypes. *See* stereotypes
Black Women Face More Trauma During Childbirth (Pearson), xiii
"Black Women Writers and the Trouble with Ethos" (Pittman), 55
Bland, Sandra, 105
Bozeman, Nathan, 19
breastfeeding, 15
breeder women, 26–27, 29, 33, 75
Britton, Earl, xvii
Brookins, Annette, xiv
Brown, Julia, 4, 6
Brown, Mike, 105
Bruce, Philip, 2
Bruneau, Thomas J., 58
Buchanan, Lindal, xviii, 56
button suture procedure experiment, 19

Caesarean delivery stories, 17, 117
calls to 911, 102
capitalism and motherhood, 52
Cartwright, Samuel, 13–14
caste system, 100
Castille, Philando, 105
castration of Black men, 32
Center for Reproductive Rights, xiv
chattel slavery: enslaved mothers, 5–7; healthy pregnancies in opposition to, 86; marriage recognition, 27; maternal care, 17; muted voices/identities, 58; power structure, 3–5; reproductive rights, 26–27; selling of slaves, 6; White mistresses in antebellum south, 1–2, 4–5. *See also* others
childbirth: author experiences, 92–95; breastfeeding, 15; COVID-19 pandemic and, 109; C-section stories, 17, 117; level of care questionnaires, 113; patriarchy controlling, 85; placenta retention, 16. *See also* Black midwifery; families; pregnancy

Children Health Insurance Program (CHIP), 112
Child Support Enforcement Act, 40
CHIP (Children Health Insurance Program), 112
Christian, Barbara, 28
Christian Recorder, 8
The Chronicle of the Discovery and Conquest of Guinea (Zurara), 12
citizenship, rights of, 23–26
class and education barriers: abortion access, 78–81; capitalism and motherhood, 52; caste system, 100; myths of White superiority, 103–104; not affecting outcomes for Black mothers, xvi; poverty, 32, 38, 39–41, 93–94
Collins, Patricia Hill, xviii, 1, 8, 28, 33, 39
community-based organizations, 112
compulsory sterilization, 30–31, 35–36, 77
computer science students, 110
"Constructing Essences" (Schmertz), 54
contraception: abortion rates and, 78; Depo-Provera, 36, 76; Enovid, 75; eugenics and, 29–32; forced sterilization, 30–31, 35–36, 77; intrauterine devices, 75–76; long-acting reversible contraceptives, 75–76; Norplant implantation, 76; SPLC lawsuit, 36
Cooper, Anna Julia, 53
Corea, Gena, 35
cotton roof, 15
cover art of pregnancy books. *See* visual images of motherhood
COVID-19 pandemic, 109
crack-addicted mothers, 41–45, 46
Crear-Perry, Joia, xviii–xix
c-section births, 17, 117
cultural gatekeepers, 70–72
culture of poverty, 38

Dalkon Shield, 75–76
Davis, Jordan, 102
Dean, Aaron, 105
Declaration of Independence, 23, 25
Depo-Provera, 36, 76
desegregation of hospitals, 89–90
devil and god terms, 56

Diangelo, Robin, 17, 59
Dill, Bonnie Thornton, 28
diversity in healthcare workforce, 109
domestic work, 28–29
dominative racism, 103
Donawerth, Jane, 52
Douglas, Stephen, 3
Douglass, Frederic, 4
Dovidio, John F., 103
Dred Scott case, 24–25
Dreher, Tanja, 61
drug abuse, 19, 41–45, 46

Eastern European slaves, 12
education spending *versus* incarceration spending, 99–100. *See also* class and education barriers
Emancipation Proclamation, 3
emergency C-section stories, 117
en caul births, 87
Enovid contraceptive, 75
ethos: about, 52; bad Black mother trope, 33, 56, 57; Black rhetoric, 54–55; of motherhood, 55–56; silencing and listening complications, 58–61; women rhetors and, 52–55
eugenics movement, 29–32
excessive force, 101, 105
experimentation on Black women, 18–19

Fairclough, Norman, 56, 70
faith in God, 6–7
families: in African villages, 50; breastfeeding, 15; family planning centers, 31; infant mortality, xv, 18, 89; juvenile justice system, 98–100; matriarch stereotype, 29–32; mothers as pillars of, 8; nuclear families, 50; unwed, welfare queen stereotype, 33–36, 75. *See also* childbirth
fertility, 14–15. *See also* breeder women; contraception
Flexner, Abraham, 86
forced sterilization, 30–31, 35–36, 77
founding fathers, 23
Freedman's Bureau Acts, 29
freedwomen in the North, 8
Fugitive Slave Acts, 24

Gaertner, Samuel L., 103
Garlic, Delia, 6
Garner, Eric, 105
Giddings, Dorothy, 2
Glass, David H., 31
Glenn, Cheryl, 58
Glymph, Thavolia, 4
god and devil terms, 56
Gone with the Wind (film), 4
Goode, Keisha, 92
granny midwives, 86, 87
grassroots organizations, 112
gun violence, 105
Guttmacher Institute, 78, 80
Guyger, Amy, 105
gynecological complications from antebellum births, 16–18
gynecological experimentation, 18–19

Hamilton, Dontre, 102
Harden-Moore, Tai, xiii, xv
Harper, Kimberly, xv, 92
Harper's Weekly, 2
Harris, Kamala, 111
Helping Moms Act, 112
herbal remedies, 87
Hewlett, Angel, 17
Hill, Anita, 59
historical and legal perspective: on abortion, 77–78; Black bodies characterized as both strong and weak, xvi; crack-addicted mothers, 41–45, 46; eugenics movement, 29–32; mammy image, 28–29, 33; matriarch image, 33; midwifery, 85–88; personhood and proslavery discourse, 23–26; reproductive rights of enslaved women, 26–29; teen mothers, 37–41; unwed, welfare queens, 33–36, 75; White women's influence on representations of Black motherhood, 1–5. *See also* chattel slavery; medical establishment
Holmes, David, 54
hooks, bell, xviii, 61, 97
hospitals, 89–90. *See also* medical establishment
Hunter, Lynette, 54
Hyde Amendment, 79
hyper-sexualized images, 37

hypervisibility of Black communities, 101

ideology and motherhood, 50–52
illegitimate children. *See* unwed, welfare queens
Immigration Act of 1924, 29
implicit bias, 110
incarceration spending *versus* education spending, 99–100, 100
infant mortality, xv, 18, 89
Ingraham, Laura, 101
insurance, xi, xv
intrauterine devices (IUDs), 75–76
invisibility of Black communities, 101
Irving, Shalon, xvi
IUDs (intrauterine devices), 75–76

James, LeBron, 101
Jean, Botham, 105
Jefferson, Atatiana, 105
Jefferson, Thomas, 14, 27
Johnson, Andrew, 3
Johnson, Kyria Dixon, xiii
juvenile justice system, 98–100

Kaepernick, Colin, 101
Kaplan, Elaine Bell, 39–41
Kendi, Ibram X., 11–12
Know Thy Self (Akbar), 5
Koerber, Amy, xviii

labor phases of childbirth, 86–87. *See also* childbirth
LARCs (long-acting reversible contraceptives), 75–76
Lay, Mary, xviii
legal perspective. *See* historical and legal perspective
Level of Care Questionnaire, 113
Lewis, Oscar, 38
Liberia's freeborn Blacks, 23
Lincoln, Abraham, 3
listening/listeners, 56–61
Little, Becky, 23
living conditions and illness, 18
Loehmann, Timothy, 105
Logan, Onnie Lee, 88, 89
Logan, Shirley Wilson, 53

long-acting reversible contraceptives (LARCs), 75–76
Lorde, Audre, xviii, 59, 61, 97
Luke, Jenny M., 90

mammy image, 28–29, 33
"man in the house rule," 32
Martin, Nin, xvi
Martin, Trayvon, 102, 105
maternal healthcare: abortion, 77–81; antebellum conditions, 16; author's experience, xi–xiii, 92–95; bias and disparity in, xiv, 73, 109–110; current access to, 95; Level of Care Questionnaire, 113; mortality rate, xiii, xiv, 8; reimagining, 109, 111–112; risk factors for illness and death, xviii. *See also* contraception; families; medical establishment; visual images of motherhood
maternal theory and ideology, 50–52
matriarchs of Black families, 29–33
media, Black mothers in, xviii, 49. *See also* visual images of motherhood
Medicaid, 112
Medical Apartheid (Washington), 13, 75
"Medical Education in American: Rethinking the Training of American Doctors" (Flexner), 86
medical establishment: during antebellum era, 13–14; bias awareness needed in, 109–110; Black midwifery competing with, 85–88; Black women as test subjects, 14, 35, 75–77; COVID-19 pandemic and, 109; disregarding Black women's experiences, xiv; diversity needed in, 109; fictitious "Black" diseases, 13; as gatekeepers, 70–71; hospital access, 89–90; pain management, xv, 13–14, 19, 91; silence of Black mothers and, 61. *See also* maternal healthcare
medical experiments, 14, 19, 35, 75–77
microaggressions, 103–104
middle-class Blacks, 41
midwifery. *See* Black midwifery
Mills, Sara, 13
Montagne, Rene, xvi
Moore, Fannie, 4, 7

Moore, Patrick, xvii
morphine addictions, 19
Morrison, Toni, xviii, 54, 69, 71–72
mortality rates, xiii, xiv, 8
motherhood. *See* Black midwifery; chattel slavery; childbirth; contraception; families; maternal healthcare; pregnancy
mourning of enslaved women, 6–7
Moynihan, Daniel, 38
Murphy, Carrie, xviii
muteness, 58–60
myths of White superiority, 103–104

narratives of mythological delusion, 103
National Origins Act, 29
natural remedies, 87
negative ethos. *See* historical and legal perspective
Negro Project, 31
"Negros and Birth Control" (Du Bois), 30
neonatal tetanus, 18
new Jim Crow, 100–101
Norplant implantation, 76
North Carolina, 80–81, 90, 91
Northern freedwomen, 8
Not Our Kind of Girl (Kaplan), 39–41
NPR stories, xv, xvi
nuclear families, 50
nurse midwives, 92–95

Ohio abortion laws, 81
"Only White Women Get Pregnant" (Harper), 92
others: Black bodies treated as, 8, 11; Black mothers as, 8, 29, 34, 73
Out of the House of Bondage (Glymph), 4
Owens, Kim, xviii

pain management, xv, 13–14, 19, 91
patriarchies, 50, 85
Payne, Hakima, xviii
Pearson, Catherine, xiii
Pendleton, E. M., 15
personhood, 23–26
Petty, Candice, 99
Phillip, Abby, 59
Pierce, Chester M., 103–104
Pierce, Dr. (obstetrician), 36

Pincus, Jane, 51
Pinto-Correia, Clara, 51
Pittman, Coretta, 55
The Pivot of Civilization (Sanger), 30
placenta retention during childbirth, 16
The Plantation Negro as a Freeman (Bruce), 2
police interactions: juvenile justice system, 98–100; racial profiling, 104–105; Starbucks calls to 911, 102; surviving, 98; violence and shootings, 104–105; White citizen police, 101–104, 105
poverty, 32, 38, 39–41, 93–94. *See also* class and education barriers; unwed; welfare queens
power: cultural gatekeepers and, 70–72; historical personhood and, 23–26; of speaking out and being silenced, 58–61. *See also* medical establishment; *others*; White privilege and power
pregnancy: ending in abortion, 77–81; fertility, 14–15; "Only White Women Get Pregnant" (Harper), 92; shame of, 77; of slaves, 27. *See also* breeder women; maternal healthcare; visual images of motherhood
prisonpolicy.org, 98
privatization of the prison industry, 100
pro-choice organizers, 81
ProRepublica, xv
public assistance, 32, 38, 39–41
publishers as gatekeepers, 71
puerperal (childbed fever), 17

racial profiling, 104–105
racial uplift, 8
racism: aversive racism, 103–104; Black midwifery and, 88; covert in school-to-prison pipeline, 98–101; dominative racism, 103; of English colonists, 11–12; implicit bias training, 109–110; as mental health illness, 104; microaggressions, 103–104. *See also* chattel slavery; historical and legal perspective; stereotypes
Ratcliff, Krista, 61
Reagan, Ronald, 39
Reconstruction exploitation, 29

reimagination of maternal health, 109, 111–112
religion, 11, 12, 41
reproductive justice, 97, 105, 110, 112
reproductive rights, 26–27, 30–31
resistance: motherhood and, 97; to police violence and profiling, 104–105; reproductive justice and, 97, 105, 110, 112; school-to-prison pipeline and, 98–101; to White citizen police, 101–104, 105
Reynolds, Nedra, 53
rhetorical tools and Black women, 53–56
Rice, Tamir, 105
rights of citizenship, 23–26
risk factors for illness and death, xviii
Roberts, Dorothy, xviii, 12, 35
Robinson, Harriet, 4
Roe v. Wade, 77–81
Rothman, Barbara, 51, 52
Ryan, April, 59

Sanger, Margaret, 30–31
Sawyer, Wendy, 98
Schmertz, Johanna, 53, 54
school-to-prison pipeline, 98–101
Schur, Richard, 54
Schwartz, Marie J., 14, 16, 17, 87
scientific racism, 12, 26
Seigel, Marika, 51
self-definition of Black women, 55
sexual relationships: controlled through AFDC rules, 32, 40; hyper-sexualized images, 37. *See also* contraception
sharecropping system, 29
Shaw, Kiana, xiv
Sheppard-Towner Maternity and Infancy Act, 88–89
silence, 56–61, 101
Simkins v. Moses H. Cone, 90
Sims, James Marion, 18–19, 35
slaves and slavery. *See* chattel slavery; Eastern European slaves
Smith, Philip W., 17
Smith, William A., 103
social justice, 110
Solozaro, Daniel G., 103
Southern Poverty Law Center (SPLC), 36
Starbucks calls to 911, 102

stereotypes: angry Black woman trope, 59; bad Black mother trope, 33, 56, 57; Black bodies, xvi, 12, 14; Black men, 2–3, 12, 14; breeder women, 26–27, 29, 33, 75; crack-addicted mothers, 41–45; ethos and, 55; mammy image, 28–29; matriarchs, 29–32; racial profiling, 104–105; teen mothers, 37–41; unwed, welfare queens, 33–36, 75. *See also* racism
sterilization. *See* forced sterilization
sterilized medical instruments, 17
"A Talk to Teachers" (Baldwin), 103

Taney, Roger, 24–25
Technical and Professional Communication (TPC), xvii, 110
technology, 51
teen mothers, 37–41
three-fifths compromise, 24
Toure, Pamela Bridgewater, 79–80
TPC (technical and professional communication) training, 110
"The Transformation of Silence into Language and Action" (Lorde), 59
"Transforming Silence" (Toure), 79–80
Trump, Donald, 59, 112
Truth, Sojourner, 7

Underwood, Lauren, xv, 111
University of Virginia study, xvi
unwed, welfare queens, 33–36, 75. *See also* Aid to Families with Dependent Children (AFDC)
U.S. government: Constitution, 24–26; Declaration of Independence, 23, 25; incarceration spending *versus* education spending, 99–100, 100; Momnibus, 111–112. *See also* historical and legal perspective

vaginal fistulas, 19
vaginal tears during childbirth, 16
van Dijk, Teun, 12
victim blaming, xviii
violence: by police, 104–105; pregnancy not protecting slaves from, 27; surviving, 98; by White citizen police, 101–104, 105; by White mistresses in

antebellum south, 4–5
"virtuousness" of White women, 2
visual images of motherhood: analysis of pregnancy books, 65–69, 67, 68; as gatekeepers of maternal health narratives, 70–72

War on Welfare, 39
Washington, Harriet A., xviii, 13, 18, 19, 75, 76, 86
Watkins, Kristin, 17
Webster, C. L., 7
welfare queens, 33–36, 75. *See also* Aid to Families with Dependent Children (AFDC)
Wendt, Jana, 71–72
When I Was a Slave (Yetman), 4
White citizen police, 101–104, 105
White Fragility (Diangelo), 59
White gaze, 69, 72
White patriarchy, 3
White privilege and power: historical perspective, 23–26; mammy image, 28–29; myth of White superiority, 103–104; Whiteness being centered, 71–72; White women and children protected by, 97. *See also* stereotypes
White women: cult of White womanhood, 1–2; ethos of, 55–56; maternal care as example of privilege, 17; mistresses in antebellum south, 4–5; racism in White nursing culture, xv; stereotypes during antebellum era, 1–2; tears of, 59–60; teen mothers in media, 37; White unwed mothers and adoption, 34
Williams, Fannie, 53
Williams, Marietta, 36
Williams, Serena, xvi
Wilson, Darren, 105
The Woman/Mother Continuum (Buchanan), 56
women's rhetorical tools, 52–56

Yanez, Jeronimo, 105
Yetman, Norman, 4
Yosso, Tara, 103

zero-tolerance policies, 98–99
Zurara, Gomes Eanes de, 12

About the Author

Kimberly C. Harper received her PhD in technical and professional discourse from East Carolina University, a Master of Science in technical and scientific communication from Miami of Ohio, and a Bachelor of Arts in English from North Carolina Agricultural and Technical State University. She is associate chair and assistant professor of English at North Carolina Agricultural and Technical State University where she directs the technical writing concentration for the Department of English. Her research examines social justice, race, and ethos within technical and professional communication, but she is also heavily interested in the rhetoric of maternal health, mental health, and hip-hop discourse, as well as Islam and birth practices. Before joining academia, Dr. Harper worked as a Technical Writer for Volvo Parts, North America and Jenzabar. She is the founder of *The Space of Grace*—a monthly podcast focusing on Black maternal health and reproductive justice. Follow her on Twitter @ronbett75 and Instagram @spaceofrjgrace.

www.ingramcontent.com/pod-product-compliance
Lightning Source LLC
Chambersburg PA
CBHW050909300426
44111CB00010B/1446